# ON EQUAL TERMS

BY THE AUTHOR OF

*The Golden Tradition: Jewish Life and Thought in Eastern Europe*
*The War Against the Jews 1933–1945*
*A Holocaust Reader*
*The Jewish Presence: Essays on Identity and History*
*The Holocaust and the Historians*

*Lucy S. Dawidowicz*

# ON EQUAL TERMS

## Jews in America
## 1881–1981

*Holt, Rinehart and Winston / New York*

Published by Holt, Rinehart and Winston,
383 Madison Avenue, New York, New York 10017.
Published simultaneously in Canada by Holt, Rinehart and
Winston of Canada, Limited.

Library of Congress Cataloging in Publication Data
Dawidowicz, Lucy S.
On equal terms.
Bibliography: p.
Includes index.
1. Jews—United States—History.   2. United States—
Ethnic relations.   I. Title.
E184.J5D33      973'.04924        82-2960
ISBN: 0-03-061658-1               AACR2

First Edition

Designer: Lucy Castelluccio
Printed in the United States of America
1  3  5  7  9  10  8  6  4  2

Originally published in the American Jewish Year Book,
1982 (Volume 82) in a somewhat different form.

ISBN 0-03-061658-1

# CONTENTS

# Contents

# PREFACE

In 1980 THE EDITORS of the *American Jewish Year Book*, the invaluable serial published by the American Jewish Committee and the Jewish Publication Society of America since 1899, invited me to write an essay on a century of Jewish history. They wished to mark the start of the mass migrations of the Jews from Eastern Europe in 1881. That essay was published in volume 82 of the *Year Book* as "A Century of Jewish History, 1881–1981: The View from America." It appears here as a self-contained work, somewhat revised and enlarged with statistics, a chronology, and a reading list.

This essay is a kind of interim report, a reflective pause in the course of my research toward a broad-gauged history of the Jews in America. Here I have marked out some of the territory and sketched the most distinctive features of the terrain. I hope that this overview will satisfy the reader's curiosity and enlarge his appreciation of the subject matter. Perhaps it will whet his appetite for the more comprehensive book to come.

LUCY S. DAWIDOWICZ

# ON EQUAL TERMS

# INTRODUCTION

ON MARCH 13, 1881, Russian terrorist revolutionaries in St. Petersburg threw a bomb that killed Czar Alexander II. That assassination set in motion a chain of events that eventually transformed the destiny of European Jews. The history of the hundred years since that fateful act, with its ensuing revolutions and wars, its economic crises, industrial innovations and scientific discoveries, its brutalities and unprecedented mass murders, radically altered the political face of the entire world. That century boasted more scientific advances than were made in all preceding centuries. In that century more than one hundred peoples emerged out of tribal communities and from under colonial rule to political independence and national identity.

During those hundred years no people or nation experienced a history of such profound traumas and transfigurations as did the Jews. Between 1881 and 1981 the Jews underwent the greatest dispersion of their millennial history in a mass migration without parallel in any people's history. In the space of those hundred years they suffered the most catastrophic destruction in their history, with statistics of annihilation overshadowing even the destruction of the Second Temple. In that century they endured cycles of distress and oppression during which they were persecuted and despised as pariahs. Yet in the same century they enjoyed cycles of prosperity and tolerance; they were accorded equality and respect as almost never before in their Diaspora history. In that century of extremes, the Jews for the first time in more than two thousand years reclaimed their political sovereignty and established the State of Israel. Yet the century marked also the nadir of Jewish historical experience. It witnessed first the dispersal of Ashkenazic Jewry and finally its destruction.

Every century has, to be sure, brought profound changes to the Jews and their society. Dispersed as they always were, they were buffeted more often than other peoples by the winds of change, the tempests of revolution, and the storms of war. In the preceding century, 1781–1881, the French Revolution and the emergence of nation-states with nationalism as their concomitant transformed Jewish society. The new nation-states tantalized Jews with the possibilities of emancipation—political equality and acceptance in the modern national polity—possibilities that in some countries took more than a half century to realize. In time emancipation weakened, though never quite undermined, the unity of the Jews as a people; it eventually rendered the concerted pursuit of common Jewish interests sometimes questionable and often impossible. The Enlightenment and the rise of modernity, which had paved the way for emancipation, launched an assault upon traditional Judaism and its institutions, damaging beyond repair the authority of the Jewish religious tradition for most Jews.

Still further back, in the hundred years between 1681 and 1781, cataclysmic events of altogether different dimensions marked the course of Jewish history: the backwash of the Sabbatian movement and its corruptive aftereffects as they were played out in the Frankist movement; the rise of Hasidism, which in time modified the character of normative rabbinic Judaism. The devastating shrinkage of the Jewish population after the Ukrainian massacres of 1648–49 was followed by an unparalleled population explosion in the next century. In that century the American Revolution heralded things to come in the New World, though in 1776 no one could have foreseen the role that the United States of America would play in the future existence of the Jews.

From their long and too often unhappy history the Jews had learned the value of migration. Beginning with the wanderings of the Patriarchs and the Exodus from Egypt, migration had been a fundamental Jewish strategy for survival, the escape valve of Jewish history. Persecuted in one place, Jews fled to another. Hounded from one land, they sought refuge elsewhere. Sometimes migration was an involuntary flight from violence and sometimes a happy delivery from oppression. More often migration was a search for opportunity and a journey to freedom. The great migration launched in 1881 by the events that followed the assassination of Alexander II eventually brought about half of the East European Jews to America. That migration also initiated the First Aliyah to Palestine. More than half a century later, those Jews who had remained in Europe and their descendants became the victims of the Third Reich's war against them. Two thirds of the European Jews—six million—were murdered during the Second World War by the Third Reich and its satellites. As we look back over the span of the century, the mass migration of the East European Jews to America that began in 1881 signified a providential course for the later survival of Ashkenazic Jewry, even though cruel persecution, wretched poverty, and ceaseless upheaval had driven them forth on their wanderings.

# I
# THE GREAT JEWISH MIGRATION, 1881–1914

# 1

# The Source:
# East European Jewry

In 1881 SOME EIGHT MILLION Jews lived in Europe—about five
million in Czarist Russia, about two million in the Austro-
Hungarian empire, a half million in Germany, over a quarter of a million in Rumania, and the rest mainly in Western
Europe. The Jews of Russia, Austria, and Eastern Prussia
were mostly descendants of Polish Jews, that is, of Jews
who had lived in the Kingdom of Poland before it had been
dismembered three times at the end of the eighteenth century by its aggressive neighbors Russia, Prussia, and Austria. Enlightened despotic monarchs ruled those three
empires with absolute power. In all three empires the Jews
were subjected to discriminatory decrees and persecution.
The Polish Jews had then numbered no more than about a
million, and more than half came under Russian rule. They
were forced to live in a "Pale of Settlement," forbidden to
move into the interior of their new countries. They were
expelled from villages and prevented from living in big cities; they were disproportionately taxed, and excluded from
occupations in which they had traditionally been engaged

for centuries. They suffered a variety of harassments and discriminatory policies that were intended to bring about their conversion or, at least for the short range, to erase their Jewish distinctiveness: compulsory long-term military service, restrictions on traditional Jewish attire, compulsory attendance at secular schools, excessive taxes on kosher meat and ritual candles, prohibitions on Yiddish and Hebrew publishing, and widespread censorship.

In Prussia and Austria, where liberal political movements and industrial modernization made more headway than in Russia, the political status of the Jews and their economic position improved in the following decades. In Russia, however, widespread illiteracy and superstition nurtured economic backwardness, and despotism reinforced political and industrial apathy. The status of the Jews—as of the whole population—even as late as 1881 could be characterized as premodern and preindustrial.

After 1855, when Alexander II ascended to the throne, the situation in Russia had begun to improve. He emancipated the peasants, reformed the system of military service, introduced economic and political reforms. The czar's innovations brought greater educational opportunity to the small, rising middle class and fostered the development of a financial and industrial elite as well as a growing class of *intelligentsia*, a Russian word to describe a university-trained intellectual elite.

Still his reforms were inadequate to the widespread destitution throughout Russia and especially to the desperate poverty of the newly liberated serfs who, unprepared occupationally for their freedom, were completely without financial and intellectual resources to find their livelihoods. The burgeoning revolutionary movement in Russia fed on the discontent of the peasants and the expanding urban proletariat, while it recruited its leaders and activists from the ranks of the intelligentsia, who were unable to find opportunities for their talents in Russia's undeveloped and provincial society.

The Jews in Russia and Congress Poland—that part of central Poland that had been formed out of the duchy of Warsaw—shared in the ferment of the time, its political upheavals, economic vicissitudes, and cultural changes. Perhaps the most striking factor of Jewish existence at that time was biological. Jewish fertility in the eighteenth and nineteenth centuries increased dramatically. The Jewish population grew tenfold under Russian rule, probably exceeding the growth rate of the non-Jews. The extraordinary rise in Jewish population was no doubt also due to the exceptionally low mortality among Jews, and to their low rate of infant mortality. That high birthrate, coupled with the low mortality, continued well into the twentieth century, with the result that the Jewish population in Eastern Europe continued to grow, despite continuing depletions by emigration.

That enormous population growth, especially in the small towns of the Russian Pale of Settlement and in the backwaters of Galicia, where industrial backwardness and primitive agriculture produced economic stagnation, sapped the economic resources of the Jews and narrowed their economic opportunities. Traditional Jewish occupations were in trade and handicrafts. The Jews were small entrepreneurs, artisans, and journeymen in the clothing crafts (tailoring, cap-, shoe-, and bootmaking, hosiery, furriery), in textile weaving, carpentry, and masonry. Jews were blacksmiths, and also goldsmiths and silversmiths. They were bakers, butchers, and vintners. They were carters, drivers, day laborers. They were innkeepers and estate managers. Eastern Europe's retail and wholesale trade, from the big grain and timber merchants down to the itinerant peddlers, was largely in Jewish hands. Jews were agents, factors, brokers for agricultural produce and manufactured goods. Intermediaries between country and city, the Jews brought the peasants' produce to the cities and delivered into the rural areas the manufactured goods that the towns and cities produced.

ALEXANDER II's REFORMS had created new opportunities for Jews. In a short time Jewish entrepreneurs, bankers, and merchants prospered and helped the Russian economy to prosper. Their usefulness was often rewarded by special privileges, including permits to live in St. Petersburg, Moscow, or other growing metropolises from which the masses of Jews were barred. In this period too, when the universities were opened to them, Jews began to enter the professions, especially medicine and law.

Until the partitions of Poland the Jews had preserved a largely autonomous social and cultural existence. Their religious, educational, and charitable institutions were maintained and directed by the kehillah, an oligarchy of wealthy and learned Jews. Originally a self-governing Jewish body, the kehillah was then undergoing a change that gravely impaired its relations with the community it regulated. Under the pressure of despotic and absolutist rulers, the kehillah was assigned tasks that were not intended to serve the needs of the Jewish community but rather to carry out the exigent demands of the oppressive regime. The czarist regime used the kehillah, for example, in the forcible recruitment, sometimes by kidnapping, of Jewish children for twenty-five-year terms of military service. The kehillah was required to impose exorbitant taxes on the Jews for kosher meat and for candles used for ritual purposes. The impoverished Jews began to regard the kehillah as an instrument of a hostile government and the consequent social tensions in the Jewish community hastened the decline of traditional authority in the Jewish community.

Early in the nineteenth century, Hasidism swept

through Jewish Eastern Europe, capturing the loyalties of most Jews, leaving embattled and embittered supporters of normative rabbinic Judaism in beleaguered urban enclaves, especially in Vilna and elsewhere in Lithuania. Hasidism constituted a social revolution as well as a religious one, by overturning the authority of the rabbis learned in Jewish law and elevating the charismatic *rebbes* and their oral teachings. In effect, Hasidism in its own way began to change the traditional structure of rabbinic authority in the Jewish community. It also brought to the little man greater awareness of his own self-worth.

The greatest assault against tradition came from the forces of secularism—the almost irresistible movement of Enlightenment, bringing secular education into a world that had been shaped and guided by Talmudic learning. Western influences penetrated into Eastern Europe, from Vienna into Galicia, from Prussia into Lithuania and Latvia. Under the influence of the Berlin Haskalah, the Jewish offshoot of the European Enlightenment, and of Moses Mendelssohn's followers, innovations began to be introduced into the *heder*, the traditional Jewish elementary school. In Riga, where German influences were strong, attempts to modernize synagogue services, to "reform" Judaism, which had been initiated in Germany early in the nineteenth century, were started, and such efforts spread to other large cosmopolitan centers with upper-middle-class Jewish elites.

The effort of Jewish enlighteners to modernize traditional Jewish institutions was in part helped but in greater part hindered by the parallel effort on the part of Nicholas I's regime to secularize the Jewish educational system at the elementary level and at its highest level—the rabbinical seminary. For the state's program was seen by the Jewish masses to be not just a step toward modernization, but a program intended to wean the Jews altogether from their religious traditions and separatist culture. Indeed its ulti-

mate purpose was to convert the Jews to the Russian Orthodox Church. Still, everywhere throughout Eastern Europe,
well-to-do Jews—merchants, bankers, industrialists, and
professionals—headed movements within the Jewish community for secular education, urging the abandonment of
Yiddish for Russian, Polish, or German. More important,
they worked to improve the economic status of the Jews by
encouraging them to enter "useful" and "productive"
occupations and by providing them with vocational and agricultural training as well as secular education in the language of the country.

In the second half of the nineteenth century a new
secularist force appeared among the Jews in the guise of the
revolutionary populist movement. Revolutionary groups
had made more headway in recruiting and organizing under Alexander II's liberal regime than they had under his
despotic predecessor. Young Jews who studied at the universities and who entered the professions, especially those
who were deeply bruised by the pariah status of Jews in
Russian society, were attracted to the revolutionary movement, for it promised to destroy the hated social order and
replace it with a new society based on equality and fraternity. Toward the end of the nineteenth century, the revolutionary movement in czarist Russia spawned separate
Jewish revolutionary movements that were not only animated by the drive to reorder Russia's social and political
structure but were specifically directed to solving the anom-
aly of Jewish existence—to make the Jews equal participants
in the larger society, yet also free to develop their own
cultural and national existence.

Anti-Semitism had been a constant in Eastern Europe.
Since the Polish partitions, restrictive and discriminating
regulations and laws were the familiar expression of that
anti-Semitism. A new phenomenon—the pogrom—man-

ifested itself first during Easter 1871 in Odessa. Odessa was the most cosmopolitan and liberal city of the czarist empire, the newest city to have been established with the least history of anti-Semitism, a place where the Jews were assimilated, Russified, and more at ease than anywhere else in Russia. That pogrom was a harbinger of things to come. It had demonstrated that the inhospitality of the czarist regime and indeed of all Russian society to the presence of Jews among them was not predicated on Jewish poverty or separatism, that even those Jews who met the criteria of the Russifiers were just as vulnerable to persecution as were the poor and unacculturated Jews.

The revolutionary terrorists who assassinated Alexander II had hoped that the anticipated czarist reprisals would spark enough revolutionary energy among the peasants to overthrow the government. But the political course took a very different direction. The new czar, Alexander III, and his advisers determined that they would restore a political order in Russia in conformance to Nicholas I's old-line, die-hard principles of "nationality, Orthodoxy, and autocracy." They hanged the terrorists and at first put the blame for the assassination on them. But very soon, in a policy of political expediency, they blamed the Jews for all of Russia's troubles. On April 16, just six weeks after Alexander II's assassination, a pogrom erupted in Yelisavetgrad, southern Russia. A wave of pogroms then inundated the Jews across all of Russia, lasting until well into 1882. The terror and the violence of the peasant mobs against the Jews equaled the devastation of war. Jewish property was plundered and destroyed; Jewish women were raped; Jewish children were mutilated; Jews were murdered. About 225 Jewish communities were affected. Some 20,000 Jews were left homeless; 100,000 were economically ruined; Jewish property valued at over $80 million was destroyed. The pogroms spread into Congress Poland, and on Christmas Day 1881 in Warsaw, where the Jews thought they lived in peace with the Poles, they were pogromized.

THE JEWS BEGAN TO FLEE from their homes and country, desperate to escape the raging violence and terror unloosed against them by the czarist regime. That precipitous and unpremeditated flight turned into a mass exodus, for even as the czarist regime stopped fomenting pogroms against Jews, it embarked on a more systematic form of persecution that could be described as an administrative pogrom. In May 1882 the infamous May Laws were enacted, designed not only to deprive the Jews of their livelihoods in Russia, but to make their continued existence altogether intolerable. The new czarist policy affected almost every aspect of the Jews' existence—their places of residence, their economic and educational opportunities, their civic status. That policy demonstrated with calculated contempt and cruelty that the Jews would have no future in Russia. Thenceforth, until the outbreak of the Great War in 1914, except only for the brief interlude of the abortive Revolution of 1905, Jewish existence in Russia was marked by cycles of violent pogroms and administrative persecution. What had begun as a stream of Jewish refugees in flight from terror in 1881 turned into a flood tide of mass migration.

The brutal bloody events of 1881 in czarist Russia overshadowed the rise of political anti-Semitism in Western and Central Europe. New political parties came into being there, especially in Germany and in Austria, that made anti-Semitism a central political issue. That departure in European politics would culminate a half century later in the destruction of the Jews. Rumania had become an independent nation in 1878 and launched its independence by pursuing a policy of systematic persecution of the Jews.

In the mind of the European Jews, America had long

been a symbol of freedom, a distant land, exotic for its Indians and black slaves, but universally perceived as a beacon of liberty and equality. Indeed America represented to the European Jews what it represented to the millions of immigrants who had come from all over Europe since the seventeenth century. It was the "New World," fresh with possibilities that no longer existed in the Old World. It was the "golden land," rich in opportunity to work, to eat, to make a better and more comfortable life for oneself than in the bleakness of the old world. America beckoned with the future, while Europe was mired in the past. Goethe's poem to the United States, written in 1827, affirmed the image of America that put in motion generations of immigrants:

> *Amerika, du hast es besser*
> *Als unser Kontinent, das alte.*
>
> America, you are better off
> Than our continent, the old one.

America offered a vision of a land without old prejudices, freed from the chains of tradition. America was without the encumbrances of the past, without the fixities of established society, without distinctions of caste and class. One of Sholom Aleichem's characters extolled America as "the only land of real freedom and of real equality. In America you can sit right here and next to you will sit the President." America, he said, was the land of opportunity: "All the millionaires and billionaires in America worked hard and long when they were young. Some in the shop and some on the street. Ask Rockefeller, Carnegie, Morgan, Vanderbilt, what they once were. Didn't they sweep the streets? Didn't they sell newspapers? Didn't they shine shoes for a nickel?"

To be sure, voices were raised that spoke of America

not as *di goldene medine*, "the golden land," but as *di treyfene medine*, "the impure land," the place where Judaism could not and did not thrive, where the Sabbath was violated, where *kashrut* and *yidishkayt* could not withstand the winds of freedom. There were even some—but not very many— who spurned America for a return to Zion. A proto-Zionist movement began to take shape in those days among young, Russified Jews whose Jewish identity had been stirred into consciousness by the pogroms. A few hundred undertook the hazardous journey to Palestine to settle in the ancestral Jewish land and to reclaim the recalcitrant soil with the labor of their own hands.

But most Jews who wanted to leave Russia, Galicia, and Rumania set their course for America. A small segment of them known as the *Am Olam* ("eternal people") shared the pioneering idealism of the early Zionists. Products of the Russian universities, imbued with populist ideas and the glorification of peasant life, they hoped to till American soil, living by the sweat of their own labor and off their own produce. But for the most part the two million Jewish emigrants from Eastern Europe who came to America between 1881 and 1914 came in search of opportunity and freedom in the New World, eager for that new start and that new life that America symbolized.

The Jews who fled their homes and towns in the Russian Pale right after the pogroms of April 1881, the impoverished Jews from the backwater towns and villages of Galicia, and the persecuted Jews of Rumania who set off on foot toward America were cut of the same cloth. They were young; at first most of them were men, later also young women joined the exodus; still later, young families began to emigrate. For the most part they were vigorous and adventurous, physically able to endure the long and difficult journey that they usually undertook with few, if any, funds. Sons and daughters left their parents behind them; they were eager to depart, ready to test their strength, to earn their independence, to enter new worlds and find new experiences. The impulse to emigrate was stimulated by the lack of opportunity and by persecution, but it had its deeper source in the restless energy of young people discontented with their lot. The discontent was, of course, greatest among the poor and the lowly. Those who owned property, who had solid occupations or who were professionals, who could maintain themselves despite the oppressive restrictions and discriminations, were the least likely to emigrate. For why abandon their homes and positions, their ties and connections? Among the discontented and the distressed, the most avid emigrants were those who wished to break away from the watchful eyes of their elders, who wished to escape the prescribed patterns of behavior set by the traditional community, who were ready to abandon the observance of the 613 commandments of Jewish law, and who resented the condescension of the Jews with status and the contempt of the Jews with learning.

These emigrants had confidence in themselves; they hoped with boundless optimism that in the New World, once they were rid of the age-old heritage of anti-Semitism, once they had jettisoned the class distinctions of the traditional Jewish community, they would be on their way to success and prosperity, to that better life toward which all Jews strove. They were characteristically the new Americans.

# 2

# The Destination:
# America and Its Jews

ALL HUMAN HISTORY can be described as a story of migration, but in the annals of history no country has surpassed the United States as the quintessential country of immigration. The United States was created, peopled, cultivated and fructified, pacified and developed, opened to trade and commerce, mechanized and industrialized, united and solidified, beautified and civilized by endless generations of its immigrants. For four centuries since the American continent was discovered, between fifty and sixty million immigrants came and most of them stayed and made their homes there.

America was shaped by three primary factors—its geography and landscape, its diverse peoples, and its Constitution. The breadth of its land and the vastness of its space with its great plains and big sky, the abundance of natural resources, lakes and rivers, woods and mountains, the rich yield of its soil—all these gave America and the new Americans an expansiveness, an openness, a freewheeling character. The immigrants' conquest of nature and of the land bred confidence and self-reliance. These new immigrants were inquisitive and pioneering, acquisitive and building, restless, always on the move, propelled by nervous energy to seize, to grasp, to make the most of America's natural wealth. They responded to the extraordinary freedom that the wilderness afforded them and that later the Constitution and government legitimated. The big country generated independence and initiative, for everything was new and nothing was settled. The society was open and fluid, without privileged classes and ascribed status. Every man could make of himself what he wished to be, to make his dreams come true and to fulfill his wildest ambitions.

FROM THE EARLIEST TIMES, the immigrants came from different places, spoke different languages, worshiped in different churches. The vast space of the country made tolerance and toleration of differences feasible, as immigrants of different ethnic origin and of dissident religious faiths settled in separate places. They established their own communities, their own forms of worship, their own social relations. In colonial times some groups sought to impose their beliefs upon others, but they did not succeed in making their views prevail, for the dissidents were able to move elsewhere, to get their own space where they could conduct their lives as they chose.

The accelerating immigration in the eighteenth century and especially in the nineteenth continued to enrich the diversity of the American population. As the frontiers receded and cities grew and became crowded, the struggle for accommodation among various groups sometimes took on violent forms that the frontier had sanctioned. Yet each new immigrant group, whether a religious or an ethnic minority, managed to wrest from the already settled majority tolerance and eventually respect, and also to hold on to those elements of its own religious and cultural tradition that it cherished. In time, for all their diversity, the immigrants learned to live together in peace, if not always in mutual regard for each other's values and customs. One dream all immigrants shared: not just to retain the essence of their identity, but to become something new—Americans.

The new federal government of the United States of America and its Constitution made it possible for everyone to become an American. The Constitution, the product of the Founding Fathers, that extraordinary assemblage of brilliant minds shaped by the European Enlightenment and tempered by the American experience, had been preceded by the Declaration of Independence. The impact of the Declaration was perhaps most dramatically described by Abraham Lincoln in his Gettysburg Address in 1863: "Four score and seven years ago, our fathers brought forth upon this continent a new nation, conceived in liberty and dedicated to the proposition that all men are created equal."

The Constitution established the legal procedures to maintain the political reality. It sought to ensure that the democracy that was a consequence of equality would not diminish any man's liberty. Thus, the Constitution combined a conservative spirit and a revolutionary one, protecting the rights and liberties of all its citizens against tyrannical government and also against a tyrannical majority. The complex political institutions, with the built-in system of checks and balances, necessary to establish justice, insure domestic tranquillity, provide for the common defense, promote the general welfare, and secure the blessings of liberty were set forth in the Constitution. Its appended Bill of Rights guaranteed to each American fundamental liberties. Of especial import for our story was the first provision in the Bill of Rights' first article: "Congress shall make no law respecting an establishment of religion, or prohibiting the free exercise thereof. . . ."

Freedom of religion for each person to worship as he chose, without the state's interference on behalf of one religion or against another, without the state's preference for one among many, was a new and revolutionary departure in eighteenth-century political thought and policy. With this clause of the Bill of Rights, the Founding Fathers set America on a new course, establishing the equality of all religions before the law and prescribing the state's indifference to the practice of religion or the neglect of it. Under the Constitution, a man's religion was no obstacle to his citizenship, no bar to his right to hold public office, no hindrance to his participation in the larger community. The Constitution of the United States thus gave to the Jews what they had been denied everywhere in Europe until then—equal citizenship, equal rights, and equal responsibilities in the state. When George Washington visited Newport on August 17, 1790, the congregation of the Newport synagogue sent him a letter of welcome. In a paragraph whose biblical rhetoric has resonated through the generations with the love that Jewish immigrants have felt immemorially for America, they said:

> Deprived as we hitherto have been of the invaluable rights of free citizens, we now—with a deep sense of gratitude to the Almighty Disposer of all events—behold a government erected by the majesty of the people—a government which to bigotry gives no sanction, to persecution no assistance, but generously affording to all liberty of conscience and immunities of citizenship, deeming everyone of whatever nation, tongue, or language, equal parts of the great governmental machine.

To be sure, many times in American history, the political reality diverged from the legal prescription of the Constitution. For several decades some states denied Jews the right to hold office. America was, despite the Constitution, in its quotidian life a Christian country. From earliest times the culture and social life of the United States were permeated by the symbols of Christianity and by the triumphalism of the church over the synagogue. American patriotism was informed by a belief in America's chosenness, by the conviction that Providence had shaped, and continued to shape, America's destiny, by the persistent identification of America with nondenominational Protestant Christianity. Yet, notwithstanding the frequently attempted encroachments by militant Protestants against the Constitutional provision separating church from state, notwithstanding the pervasive Christian religiosity in American life, the Jews in America always exercised their full rights as citizens and at the same time managed to preserve their Jewish identity. Furthermore, they were able to maintain a great network of private institutions that ensured the free exercise of their religion and their freedom to teach it to their children.

The separation of church and state produced the system of voluntarism. Members of each religious group—faith, denomination, or sect—voluntarily supported and maintained their own religious institutions without benefit of the state's financial support, political backing, or moral suasion and without hostile intervention on the part of any branch of government. Philip Schaff, the Swiss-German theologian and church historian who settled in America in the mid-nineteenth century, observed that the voluntary principle of support of religion was "truly wonderful." He noted that the multitude of churches, ministers, colleges, theological seminaries, and benevolent institutions were founded and maintained "entirely by free-will offerings," that in New York there were more and better attended churches than in Berlin, where the church was supported by the state. To be sure, the need to raise money in America for the religious institutions involved, as he saw it, "petty drudgery, vexations, and troubles," which the well-endowed established churches in Europe never knew. But the voluntary system generated interest and commitment among the laity and stimulated their involvement in religious affairs to a far greater degree than did the European system.

Separation and voluntarism legitimated religious pluralism. Though for most of the nineteenth century, evangelical Protestantism dominated what we now call America's civil religion, that is, religion as a ceremonial function in America's public life, both Roman Catholicism and Judaism succeeded, thanks to the persistence of their believers and the ethos of the Constitution, to find acceptance and respect as equal participants in the religious life in America. Thus, on February 1, 1860, when the thirty-sixth session of Congress was opened, in accordance with a long tradition, by a clergyman's invocation, that was the first time that the clergyman was a rabbi—Morris J. Raphall of Congregation B'nai Jeshurun in New York. The occasion symbolized the acceptance of Judaism as one of the three major faiths of America. To be sure, there were unfriendly gibes and even anger in some Protestant evangelical quarters because they regarded the rabbi's invocation at a national public event as a threat to their image of America as a Christian country.

The unfriendly gibes reflected the undercurrent of anti-Semitism that was present in America. Though America was new and its political institutions were new, the immigrants to America brought with them venerable traditions and hoary prejudices of their Old World. That baggage included the hodgepodge of anti-Jewish feelings, contemptible stereotypes, and religious bigotry. The new arrangements in America constantly challenged the old attitudes, and the sheer diversity of all religious groups sometimes blurred the sharp distinction between Christian and Jew. Furthermore, the philo-Hebraic strain in Puritanism bred a curiosity about real Jews that often encouraged a neutral interest in Judaism, at times even a favorable one. The evangelical strain in Protestantism intensified the conversionary activities of those churches, because of their belief that Jesus would return to earth only after all the Jews were converted. But in contrast to the Draconian attempts to convert the Jews, undertaken jointly by church and state in Austria, Prussia, and Russia, the efforts of the American missionaries were quite benign and ineffectual.

Nor was the stereotype of the Jew as Christ-killer as powerful in nineteenth-century America as it had been, and continued to be, in Europe. In the early nineteenth century the more common stereotype of the Jew in America was the image of the Jew as Shylock, the sharp cheat, the wily peddler, the dishonest merchant. That imagery was associated also with the Yankee peddler and the New England merchant. It grew out of hostility of simple rural folk toward trade and business, toward the real-life manifestations of urban civilization. Yet even this hostility that Jews encountered as businessmen and tradesmen was often mitigated by the grudging respect that they won because they worked hard, lived soberly, valued thrift, and altogether embodied the Protestant work ethic. For many of the traditional Jewish values regarding work and family life were the same values Protestant Americans cherished.

Anti-Semitism surfaced from time to time in America's political life. Yet for the most part it took the form of short-lived episodes that were challenged not only by the affected Jews, but by outraged Christians. In America, any anti-Jewish incident usually rallied non-Jews in defense of the Jews and in opposition to bigotry, a response seldom observed in

European countries. From its earliest days, America was different. Its government in fact gave no sanction to bigotry.

In 1877, on the eve of the mass migration of the East European Jews, there were nearly 250,000 Jews in the United States. About one fourth of them lived in New York City and another fourth in the rest of the North Atlantic states. Some 20 percent lived in the North Central states (especially Illinois, Missouri, and Ohio), another 20 percent in Southern and South Atlantic states (Louisiana, Maryland), and 10 percent were in the West, especially California. At that time the Jews lived in 170 communities, and maintained over 270 congregations.

In 1789 barely two or three thousand Jews lived in the new nation, whose total population then was nearly four million. Those Jews, of both Sephardic and Ashkenazic ancestry whose families had settled in colonial times in New York and Philadelphia, Charleston and Savannah, were mostly native-born, prosperous merchants, businessmen, and even professionals. In the late 1830s, Jews from Germany began to come in large numbers. They were part of a massive stream of German migration to America, prompted by the scarcity of land, rural poverty, and severe government restrictions on the right to marry, to establish domicile, and to work at various occupations. Most Jewish immigrants came from small towns in Baden, Bavaria, Württemberg, and Bohemia, and also from Prussian Posen, which had been part of Poland until the partition of 1793. The Posener Jews have been counted among the German Jews, but they were in fact Polish Jews and were a vanguard of the later East European migration.

For the most part, the immigrants from the German-speaking lands were youngsters, teenagers, without resources other than their youth and vigor and their Jewish ties, which stood them in good stead. The informal network of support and encouragement that existed among Jews functioned like an extended family. Not only did cousins and more distant relatives help each other, but the support system applied also to Jews from the same community, the same region, to Jews who spoke the same language, and indeed to all Jews.

Along with the Irish and German immigrants, the Jewish immigrants kept coming. By 1840, 15,000 Jews were already in the United States. Twenty years later, on the eve of the Civil War, their numbers had reached about 150,000, the tenfold growth accounted for mainly by immigration rather than by natural increase. After 1848, following the failed revolution in Germany and the subsequent political reaction, the character of the Jewish immigrants changed somewhat. Those disappointed Jews who had hoped in 1848 for a better life in their own land now embarked for America. They were somewhat older than the first wave of German Jewish immigrants, though the young still predominated among them. They were also more educated. Most German Jewish immigrants had from the start come from pious homes, but had had few opportunities for education, either general or Jewish. The Polish Jews who came from Posen had more Jewish education and were more likely to know a trade than the Jews who came from the small German market towns.

Those Polish Jews who came in the 1840s and 1850s, like the Polish Jews who would come fifty years later, worked at trades they had followed in the old country—as tailors and shoemakers, as merchants in dry goods and secondhand clothing. Most German Jewish immigrants, without training or experience, took to peddling as their means of support. They needed no capital for peddling, often able to get their first small stock on credit from relatives or friends or by helpful contacts through the Jewish community. In those days the itinerant peddler was a vital link in

26

the developing commerce of the country, the intermediary between the city's manufactured goods and the farmers and homesteaders who needed those goods. Basing themselves in a city—New York or Cincinnati, St. Louis or New Orleans—where they obtained their supplies, they radiated out with their backpacks on rural routes for a week at a time. As they prospered, they bought horses and wagons, enlarged their stocks, and expanded their territory. When they accumulated enough savings, they opened stores, sometimes in the city from which they had started, sometimes in small towns out in rural areas. Jewish mercantile success was rapid, for these peddlers, storekeepers, and merchants were providing commercial services that the expanding country required. As the frontier moved westward, so did the Jews, and everywhere they made their mark. By 1858, Jewish merchants in San Francisco had become so significant an element in the city's commercial and business life that when the weekly sailing of the mail boat that year fell on Yom Kippur, the boat's departure was delayed until the next business day.

The opening up of the West accelerated the expansion of the economy. The production of manufactured goods, which had begun as so-called cottage industry, grew with the population, and the distribution system grew more complex. Retailers became producers, manufacturers; salesmen became wholesale distributors. The system of mutual trust that existed among the Jews served them in business matters as in communal affairs. The family was often the basic business unit. Some family members stayed in New York, where they produced goods—coats or collars, ribbons or umbrellas. Other family members settled in New Orleans, St. Louis, Chicago, or San Francisco, shipping, distributing, retailing. They hired from among their friends, acquaintances, and landsmen the staffs they needed: shop workers, clerks, bookkeepers, salesmen. The trade network created a demand for brokers, factors, commission merchants.

This wave of immigration coincided with the early development of the United States beyond the Appalachians, into the Middle West, the South, and the Far West. The Jews, given the wide range of their mercantile activities, served that expansion, helping to unite the vast continent with a web of commercial connections that stimulated the further growth of American business and industry. Despite hardships and frequent setbacks—robberies, fires, shipwrecks, Louisiana's yellow fever—these immigrants prospered. Some of them rose from rags to riches; most attained the modest comfort of a middle class.

Wherever the immigrants settled, they formed a Jewish congregation if none yet existed. Sometimes they rented quarters for their first High Holy Day services; sometimes they first bought land for a cemetery. Their Jewish commitments were fundamental; they carried their sense of Jewish belongingness wherever they went, even if they lapsed conspicuously from the norms of Jewish observance that they had kept in the old country. Living on the move, among strangers, they found it hard to observe the laws of *kashrut*, to maintain the sanctity of the Sabbath, to study Torah. Caught between the demands of making a living and the exhilarating freedom to do as they pleased without being judged, most of them yielded to expediency. Yet they clung to their identity as Jews, clustered wherever and whenever possible with Jews, and tried to retain whatever of their religious traditions and institutions they could accommodate to their new circumstances.

Until the 1840s there were no ordained rabbis at all in the United States and very few Jews who were at all learned in the Talmud and the other fundamental texts of Judaism. In 1840 Abraham Rice arrived: a Talmudist who had been head of a small yeshiva in a German town. Then forty years

old, already set in his ways, he became rabbi of an observant congregation in Baltimore. But his rabbinic career in
America failed. Though his congregants—peddlers and
shopkeepers—considered themselves pious Jews, their standards of observance did not satisfy Rice. He insisted on
interpreting Jewish law with rigidity, on not taking advantage of the flexible limits of the law so that it could bend a
little with conditions in America. His attitude put him on a
collision course with the congregants, and some years later
he left the congregation to become a shopkeeper. His loyalty to a maximalist interpretation is reputed to have set a
standard for Orthodox observance that still exists in Baltimore, but his tenure as rabbi had practically no noticeable
impact on the Baltimore Jewish community or on the practice of Judaism in America at large.

The first traditional Jew who understood the nature of
America's challenge to Judaism was Isaac Leeser (1806–
1868). Leeser came from a small town in Western Germany
to Richmond in 1824, when he was not yet eighteen, having
some general and yeshiva education behind him. He was to
become the most knowledgeable of the "ministers" who
served American Jewish congregations as leaders of their
prayer services and as preachers, educators, and communal
spokesmen. He became the American spokesman for traditional Judaism, taking as the model for his traditionalism
Samson Raphael Hirsch, the German rabbi who first formulated the doctrine of *Torah im derekh eretz*, that is, Torah together with secular knowledge. Leeser published a monthly
called *The Occident*, whose very name expressed his view
about the Westernness, that is, the modernity of Judaism.
Like Hirsch, Leeser believed that the traditional Jew should
become part of the larger society, though not at the expense
of his Judaism. The American Jew, he held, could loyally
observe Judaism, while he could also benefit from secular
education and participate in the civic life of his new coun-

try. As minister of the influential Congregation Mikveh Israel of Philadelphia, Leeser achieved a national reputation, and his paper gave him a national following. He prepared a wide variety of Jewish educational books. His prayer books consisted of the traditional service according to the Sephardic rite, with an English translation of both the liturgy and the biblical portions. These volumes were pioneering efforts of lasting value, still in use in some Orthodox synagogues today. He was the strongest force among American Jews in defense of traditional Judaism.

But Leeser could not stem the sweeping tide of Reform Judaism that soon captured most of the fifty American congregations established by 1850. For all the rabbis after Rice who came to America in the 1840s and 1850s were committed to Reform Judaism as they had seen it develop in Germany.

THE MOVEMENT to reform synagogue services had been started in Hamburg by lay people. But soon young rabbis, eager to revise traditional Judaism to fit the "spirit of the times," took up the question of reform more systematically. The originating impulse that underlay the drive for reform derived from the ambition and indeed the hope of the secularly educated, upwardly mobile Jews in Berlin and other German cities to win civic equality and social acceptance in German society. They regarded traditional Judaism as a backward supernatural religion that enforced Jewish separatism through its multitude of commandments and they blamed it for the anti-Jewish prejudices rampant among Germans. For their part, these modern Jews favored "natural" religion or a "religion of reason."

The innovations that the reformers introduced in the synagogues may be fairly characterized as the Protestantization of Jewish worship: German was substituted for Hebrew in the liturgy; the rabbi preached a sermon in German (preaching had never been part of the Sabbath services); certain portions of the liturgy that offended their modern sensibility were omitted; certain synagogue customs were dropped; organ music and female choirs were introduced. Family seating eliminated the separate women's section of the synagogue.

In very short order, these changes were introduced in the American synagogues. The pioneer of Reform Judaism in America and its most vigorous advocate was Isaac Mayer Wise (1819–1900), who came to the United States in 1846 and for more than a half century dominated the Reform movement and its institutions. Wise and the other Reform rabbis instituted in their synagogues those changes in the liturgy and the service that they had admired in Germany. Thereby they legitimated also the lapses in observance by the laity in their own pragmatic accommodation to Jewish law. The introduction of Reform innovations often alienated traditionalist congregants who, even if they did not themselves observe all Judaism's commandments, nevertheless wished their rabbi and synagogue to do so. Congregations split over questions like mixed seating and the introduction of the organ, yet before long there were no more than a dozen or so major synagogues that had managed to hold out against the changes of Reform.

Reform Judaism made more conquests in the United States than it did in Germany and it introduced more radical changes than were generally accepted in Germany. Reform's success in nineteenth-century America may be credited in part to its compatibility with the American scene, especially with developments among Protestants. The most vigorous Protestant denominations then in America had grown out of the English dissenting churches, which had repudiated European Christian orthodoxies and the authority of established churches. These churches, it turned out, were best adapted to survive under the rigors of life on the frontier or the vast prairie.

Few learned ministers or theologians were available to guide these Methodists, Baptists, Presbyterians, evangelicals, and revivalists, even if they would have wanted such guidance. These men had already learned to depend upon themselves not only in their struggle with the wilderness, but in their encounter with God. For them the Bible sufficed as the word of God. The Bible became their ultimate authority and they required no mediating or interpreting minister. They conducted their own services and allowed their religious feelings full and free expression. These religious feelings became the hallmark of frontier revivalism and evangelism, the articulation of which these frontier Christians believed to be a more authentic faith than the rituals of the established churches. This freewheeling individualist religion owed much to America's political ethos, which declared that all men were created equal. The self-taught man regarded himself as as good as the learned man. That ethos infected also the Jews, who having left behind them in the Old Country the distinctions of class and status, were happy no longer to have to endure their indignities. In America, where their private and public conduct could no longer be monitored as it had been in the closely knit communities of small towns, Jews became their own authorities also with regard to Judaism, deciding which commandments they would or could observe and which they would discard. The rabbis who shaped Reform movement legitimated the conduct of the lay people.

Reform's success must also be credited to the fact that in the United States there was no sufficiently strong bulwark of traditional Judaism to withstand Reform's onslaughts. There were no venerable institutions of Jewish learning and no great Talmudists who commanded sufficient authority to retard, if they could not altogether halt, the pace of Reform, which often meant the abandonment of traditional observance. This absence of traditionalist brakes in America facilitated Reform's headlong rush into radical change. Radical Reform, which in Germany established itself only in an enclave in Berlin, swept over the United States. It repudiated the whole system of Jewish law, including *kashrut*, and declared that only Judaism's moral laws were binding. It rejected the concept of Jews as a nation, asserting that they were merely a religious community and that their religion was a universal religion of reason, in harmony with the advances of science. Eventually these extreme views were incorporated in a declaration of principles adopted by a group of Reform rabbis at a meeting in Pittsburgh in 1885. Though this declaration, which became known as the Pittsburgh Platform, was never formally endorsed by the Central Conference of American Rabbis (the association of Reform rabbis founded four years later), and though moderate Reformers opposed it, it remained the emblematic statement of Reform Judaism until it was superseded in 1937 by the Columbus Platform.

WHEN THE IMMIGRANT JEWS first formed congregations in the New World, they made them in the image of the Old World. Yet the evolution of Jewish communal institutions in the United States proceeded along lines substantially different from their European counterparts. To begin with, in America participation in any Jewish institution was entirely voluntary. In Europe, to the contrary, every Jew upon birth became a member of the Jewish community, a formal body with legal standing whose status was regulated by the government. The Jewish community, called variously *kehillah, kahal, Gemeinde, gmine*, supervised a host of institutions and services to the local Jewish population—synagogues, cemetery, ritual slaughter, the ritual bath, religious education, and charity. As recently as the late nineteenth century a Jew could disaffiliate himself from the Jewish community only by renouncing Judaism and becoming a Christian. To be a Jew then was a formal and legal ascription required by governing authorities. In America, in contrast, a Jew decided for himself freely and voluntarily whether he wished to associate himself with other Jews in joint endeavors that would strengthen and enhance Judaism and help his fellow Jews in need.

When the first congregations were formed, members took upon themselves those obligations to provide the functions that had been the province of the European Jewish community organization. They bought land for a cemetery. They provided, within the limits of their resources, education for the children. They supervised ritual slaughter to provide kosher meat. They built a ritual bath. They dispensed charity to the needy.

The new immigrants who kept arriving formed their own congregations after a while, the Germans preferring their kind of service to that of the English Jews, the Polish Jews splitting off from the Germans, the Bohemian Jews maintaining their own style. Each congregation at first tried to provide those who turned to them for charity with such services as it supplied to its own members. But the growing immigration soon imposed demands for aid that outstripped the capacity of these small charitable institutions to provide.

In the 1840s a few charitable groups in New York that had originated in congregational activity merged to form a single organization and began to operate independently of the synagogue. A new pattern of Jewish communal life was in the making: philanthropic societies, unconnected with the synagogue, served Jewish communal interests, secular in purpose and program. In time their devotion to helping fellow Jews provided an institutional alternative to the synagogue for those Jews whose sense of obligation to the Jewish community was better satisfied by philanthropic work than by religious observance.

Voluntary associations proliferated all over the United States, a phenomenon that Alexis de Tocqueville had observed in 1831: "Americans of all ages, all conditions, and all dispositions constantly form associations." In 1843 the B'nai B'rith was founded as a Jewish fraternal order. The new group's purpose, as described in its constitution, evoked the traditional functions that in earlier times—in both the United States and in traditional society in Europe—had been performed by *hevras*, mutual-aid societies: "visiting and attending the sick," "protecting and assisting the widow and orphan." But the B'nai B'rith was in fact more nearly a Jewish counterpart of those fraternal orders that then flourished in America, the earliest and foremost among them the Freemasons.

From colonial times on, Jews had belonged to Masonic lodges, but beginning in the 1840s and more especially in the 1850s, as the Christian revivalist movement intensified, many Masonic lodges began to describe themselves as Christian. Jews then looked for alternatives. The B'nai B'rith began as a Jewish secret-order society, with rites and regalia, providing a social milieu for relaxed fellowship as well as mutual aid. In later decades, many other Jewish fraternal orders were formed, though none had the long life or the huge national membership that the B'nai B'rith eventually attained.

As the Jewish population grew, other types of associations came into being. As early as 1850 a Young Men's Hebrew Literary Association was founded in Philadelphia, and similar cultural groups sprouted in many cities. German Jews, living in a German-language milieu, often took part in German choral and literary societies, but as the German speakers became English speakers with the passing years, the vitality of these societies declined. The new model for cultural and social activities became the Young Men's Hebrew Association, the first one set up in Philadelphia in 1874, as the Jewish equivalent of the Young Men's Christian Association that had been founded two decades earlier.

American Jews tried to organize also a national group that could represent all Jews, but had less success. Such efforts were made especially at those times when American Jews wished to help Jews who were suffering persecution abroad. The first such cause that rallied American Jews was the Damascus blood libel of 1840, when the Jews there were accused of using Christian blood for Passover. Many Jews were arrested and tortured and the whole community was pogromized. Many congregations organized protest meetings and wrote to the President and the State Department on behalf of the Jews in Damascus. An attempt to coordinate these activities was made without result. But in 1859 the Board of Delegates of American Israelites was established, patterned after the Board of Deputies of British Jews. In the mid-1850s, when the United States had signed a commercial treaty with Switzerland, American Jews protested strongly because the Swiss distinguished prejudicially between Jews and non-Jews. (Shortly thereafter, the Swiss rescinded that distinction.) The Mortara affair of 1858, involving the forced conversion and kidnapping of a Jewish child from his home in Bologna, rallied Jews everywhere in the world, though to no eventual effect, for papal authorities refused to return the child to his family. That case united Jewish congregations in joint activity. The outcome was the formation of the Board of Delegates, a union of some thirty predominantly traditionalist congregations. (In France, the Alliance Universelle Israélite was founded in 1860, also as a consequence of the French Jews' involvement in the Mortara case.) Twenty years later the Board of Delegates was absorbed by the Union of American Hebrew Congregations, which Isaac Mayer Wise had founded in 1873. Thus Reform and traditionalist congregations joined together as one body to speak on behalf of American Jews.

THE CIVIL WAR, America's greatest trauma, created deep rifts not only between North and South, black and white, but altogether sharpened tensions in the American population. The mild forms of anti-Semitism that had existed in the Christian rhetoric of the evangelicals, in the xenophobic and anti-Catholic Know-Nothing movement of the 1840s and 1850s, and in unflattering and hostile stereotypes disseminated by the press of Jews as greedy cheating Shylocks, hardened into vicious and sometimes violent anti-Semitism in both the North and the South during the Civil War.

Jews were frequently accused of lack of loyalty, whether to the cause of the Union or the Confederacy; they were charged with evading military service, with not wanting to fight. Their major role in commerce and trade and especially in the cotton trade exposed them to ugly accusations of war profiteering and disloyalty. In many Southern towns Jewish merchants were vilified, their stores raided, and there were some cases where they were expelled from town. The most famous and infamous episode was that of General Ulysses S. Grant's Order No. 11, issued December 17, 1862, which ordered the Jews "as a class of people" to be expelled from the area under the jurisdiction of the Union Army's Department of Tennessee. Jews were physically uprooted in at least three communities (Paducah, Kentucky; Holly Springs and Oxford, Mississippi). Some Jewish representatives managed to reach President Lincoln with their protest and outrage and succeeded in getting the

President to instruct the general-in-chief of the army to have Grant rescind that order. By January 7, 1863, Grant did so.

After the war, a considerable number of Jewish merchants in the South moved away, some because they could no longer tolerate living among people who had treated them with unprecedented bigotry, others because the war's devastation had forced them to seek more favorable conditions for making a living.

The Civil War left deep wounds in the Union's body politic that took many generations to heal, and have not yet been forgotten. The Civil War also left the festering sore of anti-Semitism. The outpouring of anti-Jewish sentiments and the hostile acts against Jews in the charged atmosphere of the Civil War seemed to have sanctioned public expression of anti-Jewish sentiments in the decades that immediately followed the end of the war.

During Reconstruction (1865–1877), the United States experienced enormous economic, social, and political changes. The American economy underwent enormous expansion. In 1860 there were thirty thousand miles of railroads; the mileage doubled in a decade and trebled by 1880. Transportation facilitated the growth of industry as well as the expansion of trade. The invention of the telephone in 1874 would in a short while revolutionize communication. Inventions and technological improvements stimulated manufacturing to new levels. The steel industry boomed with the new Bessemer process (1866). Oil drilling increased and as new oil sources were found, petroleum refining became a major industry. Coal and iron production soared.

The unprecedented demands that the Civil War had created for uniforms and military supplies led the way to industrial standardization and mass production of manufactured goods. Wool production and textile weaving were accelerated by the introduction of new machinery. Between 1859 and 1869 the number of American manufacturing establishments nearly doubled as did the value of their manufactured goods. Domestic trade flourished and, even more important for America's rapidly expanding economy, export trade (especially grain, petroleum, machinery) increased.

Jews had a great share in this economic and industrial boom. The success that many German Jewish immigrants enjoyed became marked during the years of Reconstruction as the Lehmans, Strauses, Seligmans, Guggenheims, and other less famous names made great fortunes and became part of America's business elite. Less dazzling but no less visible was the widespread financial success in the 1870s of the German Jews who had arrived penniless in the 1840s and 1850s and had now achieved solid middle-class status.

Reconstruction was also a period of intense social division and bitter racial hatred. The Thirteenth, Fourteenth, and Fifteenth Amendments to the Constitution, which prohibited slavery and ensured equal civil rights to blacks, were ratified between 1865 and 1870. In blind hatred against black emancipation and against the Radical Reconstruction wing of the Republican Party, the Ku Klux Klan was founded in 1866 to restore "white supremacy." Its lawless violence soon attracted national attention. A congressional investigation led to the enactment of anti-KKK laws in 1870 and 1871, which enabled the President to use the army to combat their illegal violence; President Grant actually did use that power against the Klan. Within a short time, the Klan disappeared from the political scene. (A new KKK, patterned on this one, emerged in 1915.) The Klan's bigotry, however, persisted for generations, erupting from time to time in incidents of violence. Meanwhile, in the West racial bigotry was directed against the Chinese in riots during the 1870s, after the Chinese were permitted to immigrate to the United States. That opposition led to the passage of the Chinese Exclusion Act in 1879.

In this period of racial tensions, as the business boom gave way to the Panic of 1873, anti-Semitism intensified. Even before the panic, the enactment of the Coinage Act early in 1873, making gold the sole monetary standard, gave rise to charges of a "gold conspiracy," and for about two decades populist politicians and preachers made that monetary policy a political issue. The Greenback Labor party was founded in 1877 to rally labor support for the traditional agrarian antibanking views. The rhetoric of that movement increasingly took on an anti-Jewish character, with its references to "usurers," "money lenders," and "international bankers." "Wall Street Jews" became a frequent epithet.

Social discrimination against the Jews had existed even before the Civil War. As the Jews became prosperous enough to take vacations at seaside hotels, they found that they were not always welcome. In time, Jews built up their own resort areas where they felt comfortable, such as Long Branch, New Jersey. Jews of high status continued, however, to seek out the fashionable hotels of America's top society. But even they began to feel the chill of social exclusion as the United States entered the Gilded Age (1877–1900), the decades of flamboyant wealth and social climbing, when the ambitious new social and economic elite tried to establish its claim to fashionable society as the old gentry was losing its status. The most famous and dramatic case of social discrimination was that of Joseph Seligman, financier and friend of President Grant, who was turned away from the Grand Union Hotel in Saratoga in 1877. The middle-class Jews of America regarded that insult to Seligman as an affront to themselves, and soon the Jews launched a boycott against A. T. Stewart Company, a wholesale merchandiser, whose president had decided that "Israelites as a class" should be excluded from his hotel.

Despite the Panic of 1873, America continued to draw emigrants from Europe because of its great economic opportunities. Among the hundreds of thousands of newcomers who arrived each year between 1870 and 1880, there were also an estimated 41,000 Russian Jews, over and above the continuing flow of German Jews. By 1881 about 280,000 Jews lived in the United States. They maintained over 270 major congregations. The more recent accretion of observant Jews sustained about a dozen Orthodox synagogues, besides some fifty small congregations of new immigrants clustered mostly on New York's Lower East Side. The Reform movement had meanwhile established a major institution of higher learning, a rabbinical college and seminary to train native American rabbis. It was called Hebrew Union College and was the creation essentially of Isaac Mayer Wise.

In the years since the Civil War the network of Jewish philanthropic institutions had grown. Jewish hospitals, charitable organizations, and a host of fraternal and social groups dotted the map of Jewish communities throughout the country. These institutions, which had taken root in American soil, had their origins for the most part in traditional European Jewish society, yet they all emerged as distinctly American as they were uniquely Jewish, an embodiment of Jewishness and Judaism finely attuned to America, while firmly attached to the fundamental precept that all Jews are brothers and responsible for each other.

# 3

## *America: The Immigrant Crucible*

HECTOR ST. JOHN CRÈVECOEUR, a French farmer who lived in New York during the 1770s, wrote about his adopted country: "Here individuals of all nations are melted into a new race of men, whose labors and posterity will one day cause great changes in the world." Some 125 years later, observing the teeming immigrant population in America's big cities, Israel Zangwill celebrated America as "God's crucible, the great Melting Pot where all the races of Europe are melting and re-forming."

The concept of America as a melting pot that blended the racial and cultural ingredients of all America's immigrants to produce homogeneous Americans has lately been easily demolished by sociologists and philosophers as a crude and inaccurate description of the more complex process of assimilation. Yet undeniably America, on the frontier as in the urban slums, transformed the immigrants of foreign tongues and alien cultures into Americans. Within a brief span of time, these people of diverse stocks came to share with each other a greater devotion to their new country than they would ever again feel for their old one. The immigrants wanted to be Americans and they shed their foreign characteristics as soon as they began to feel at home in America.

To be sure, all America's immigrants retained strong ties of kinship and affection with their families and communities back in the Old Country. Immigrants from the same town and country, speaking the same language, clung to each other in the unfamiliarity of America. They settled together, built their houses of worship together, organized mutual-aid societies, and tried to transmit to their children growing up in America without Old World memories a sense of their own cultural heritage. But they never hoped merely to transplant in America the world they had left behind. What they wanted was to retain their individuality and ancestral identity at the same time they were becoming Americans.

America was also another sort of crucible. The farmers and peasants, workers skilled and unskilled, raw youths without trade or schooling were absorbed into America and most became, if not in their own lifetime then a generation later, part of middle-class America. The promise of American democracy and egalitarianism was that any penniless immigrant could make it, that everyone could become a part of middle-class America. Consequently the pressure to become American and Americanized was self-generated, for it was motivated by the ambition to become well-to-do and successful.

The immigrants were also subject to external pressure from Americans already here, from those who perhaps only a generation earlier had themselves been immigrants. From earliest times, Americans thought of their country as a haven for the oppressed of the world; they welcomed immigrants. But they expected the new immigrants to become Americans. In 1819 John Quincy Adams described America's expectation of the immigrants as he saw it: "They must cast off the European skin, never to resume it. They must look forward to their posterity rather than backward to their ancestors."

The ideal American conformed to the model of Washington, Jefferson, and Lincoln. To be an American from the first meant to swear allegiance to the flag and to uphold the Constitution. It meant also to speak English and to worship God, preferably a Protestant God. The first to feel the whiplash of that Anglo-American Protestantism were the Irish Catholics who brought into the United States a religious culture that did not conform to the Anglo-American norm. As early as the 1830s there were some Americans who wished to restrict immigration so as to bar Catholics. But however strident their voices, they were not heeded. The United States retained its open-door immigration policy, at least for the Europeans.

From the late 1830s to 1881 most immigrants to America had come from Western and Northern Europe—England, Scotland, Ireland, Germany, and the Scandinavian countries, an immigration later to be characterized as the "Old Immigration." But from 1881 to 1914 the immigrants came predominantly from Eastern and Southern Europe—Italy, Russia, Austria-Hungary, Rumania, and the Balkan countries, to be characterized as the "New Immigration." In those thirty-three years from 1881 to 1914, when immigration to the United States reached its highest levels, nearly 23 million aliens entered America. Among them were close to 2 million Jews, mostly from Eastern Europe, about 9 percent of all immigrants.

The sheer volume of the New Immigration and its overwhelming foreignness set off fears and prejudices among Americans, even among those who had themselves once been the victims of similar fears and prejudices. The New Immigrants were largely Catholic. They were penniless and propertyless; most were displaced landless peasants, with a high rate of illiteracy, without trades or skills. The East Europeans came from countries that were at that time breeding revolutions and revolutionaries, and native Americans feared their dangerous influence. The Haymarket affair in Chicago in 1886, when German anarchists threw a bomb killing seven policemen and injuring many more, confirmed the fears of Americans that the labor unrest and violent strikes in the country were fomented by foreign troublemakers. In 1901 a Polish anarchist assassinated President McKinley, reinforcing the stereotype of foreigners as anarchists.

Assertive American nationalism grew in the 1880s into the 1890s and reached a high point during the Spanish-American War of 1898. At the same time social Darwinist and racist notions imported from Europe began to influence those Americans already fearful of what they regarded as the alien hordes descending upon their country. They believed that the New Immigrants would produce racial degeneration in the American people and undo everything that America stood for. In this encompassing xenophobia a particular vein of anti-Jewish hostility was embedded, especially evident among the patricians. Thus Henry James on a visit to New York in 1904 was repelled by "a Jewry that had burst all bounds," by the phantasmagoric portent "of the Hebrew conquest of New York."

In 1894 the Boston Brahmins, the custodians of Anglo-American culture, founded the Immigration Restriction League, whose purpose was to alert the country to what they considered the threat that the New Immigrants posed to America's essential character and cultural entity. Congress had already enacted a law in 1891 placing immigration under federal authority and, augmenting a law of 1882 that had denied admission to convicts, lunatics, idiots, and persons likely to become public charges, further excluded polygamists and persons suffering from contagious disease. (In 1903 anarchists and advocates of the violent overthrow of the U.S. government were excluded.) The idea of excluding aliens illiterate in their own language was vigorously pursued by the Immigration Restriction League and Congress enacted such a bill in 1896, though President Cleveland vetoed it. The opponents of immigration, soon joined also by the labor unions fearing alien competition, continued their efforts to enact restrictive legislation, but not until 1917, shortly before America's entry into World War I, did they succeed in enacting a literacy requirement for all immigrants.

THE JEWS FROM Eastern Europe poured into America. Continuing discriminatory legislation and harsh economic conditions drove them from Russia, Austria, and Rumania. In 1903 the Kishinev pogrom in Russia launched a new exodus, and after the abortive Revolution of 1905, the ensuing reaction and the new wave of pogroms throughout Russia gave rise to further waves of migration.

Enduring the ordeals of the Atlantic passage in steerage and the humiliations of Ellis Island, they streamed into the cities, mostly New York, but also Philadelphia and Chicago. Looking for work, joining relatives, some went to Boston or Baltimore; others farther west than Chicago. They swarmed into the tenement slums of the older parts of the city, living in poverty and privation. They had arrived as a nondescript lot occupationally. (Many Jewish immigrants reported to the immigration inspectors that tailoring was their trade, but it is now generally held that their answers reflected aspiration rather than experience.) But within a few years these unskilled and inexperienced immigrants were proletarianized, turned into workers in the sweatshops of the needle trades and other light industry in New York and the other big cities. (Their entry into the needle trades was facilitated by the large number of Jewish employers.) Those who didn't work in the sweatshops took to peddling and pushcarts. A relatively small proportion had to turn to charity for help. Some immigrants were sick and could not work. Some were women with children whose husbands had deserted them. In bad economic years, when unemployment was rife, more immigrants needed help than in the better years.

These Jewish immigrants were the classic greenhorns. Three types of greenies could be distinguished among these teeming masses. The rawest among them were the *shvitsers*, the hustlers, driven by the desire to find gold in the streets of New York. They had already jettisoned whatever traditions they had grown up with. They were without binding ties to the past, without commitment to Jewish tradition. They were the hustlers and the hard workers, on the lookout for opportunities to make money, to get ahead. They progressed from sweated worker to sweater, from subcontractor to contractor, from jobber to manufacturer. They advanced from peddler to shopkeeper, from distributor to wholesaler. They were the entrepreneurs. Interested only in making money, they were usually indifferent to the Jewish community and to the observance of Judaism. In a decade or so they emerged as the *alrightniks*, satisfied with their accomplishments and accumulations.

Another type of greenhorn was the observant Jew who tried to transplant his East European practices and institutions in the new milieu. Such immigrants often shunned the sweatshops, preferring sweated home labor where they could observe the Sabbath. Or they chose to peddle or sell from a pushcart. By 1888 such Jews had established at least 130 different congregations in New York. Several of these, against advice from those who understood America better than they, imported from Vilna a learned rabbi to serve as New York's chief rabbi. They expected to finance his rabbinate through the imposition of tax on kosher meat. The very idea that a chief rabbi could operate authoritatively in the chaos of New York's uncontrolled freedom revealed how green these observant Jews were. Such an institution, subsidized by such an unpopular tax, had indeed been the practice in Eastern Europe, where it worked mainly because the kehillah functioned under governmental authority. In New York, the kosher meat industry was rife with corruption and scandal, always difficult to regulate and supervise. As predicted, the grandiose idea for the functioning of the chief rabbi failed. The rabbi lived in poverty and even scorn until his death in 1902.

The pious Jews attempted to transplant the *heder*—private Jewish elementary school—and the Talmud Torah—a community school—to America, but at best they could operate only as supplementary schools to the public schools. Even so, they were unattractive. The children of the pious Jews themselves fled the dreariness and the Old World rigidity of those Jewish schools, making fun of their greenhorn teachers, those *melamdim* who continued to use the old methods of teaching children by rote. The Jewish children grew up on the street, tempted by American freedom, drawn to the public schools, to games, to baseball, to sports. Indeed, most immigrant Jews looked to the public schools to teach their children to become Americans. From the start they saw the school and the education it offered as the vehicle promising success in the big world outside.

The third type of greenhorn was the radical, the freethinker who wished to transplant his political ideology in America. Socialists, anarchists, syndicalists, and combinations thereof, they came with ideas and ambitions shaped by the tyranny of absolutism, of reaction, of pogrom. They looked at America and its political institutions through the distorting glass of East European politics. They were absorbed for nearly two decades in theoretical questions of radical politics that had little relevance to the lives of the immigrant Jews. They dissented from one another, fragmenting their movements into quarreling factions. They aggressively attacked the "clericalism" of traditionalist Jews, ridiculed their observances, and instituted the Yom Kippur balls, a public mockery of Judaism's most sacred holy day. The East Side radicals made little headway in the first two decades of mass migration, unable to agree among themselves as to the nature of the revolution to come and unable to understand the needs and interests of the Jews around them.

Probably most of the East European immigrants living in the slums of the industrial cities at that time combined a little of each of these greenhorn types. Not all of them shared the single-minded intentness of the *shvitser* to make money. Yet they all wanted to get ahead and most of them eventually did or saw to it that their children did. By far not all of them shared the determination of the observant Jews to hold fast to Judaism as they had practiced it in the Old Country. Yet on the High Holy Days great numbers went to services. Most immigrants bought kosher meat, if they no longer observed the other laws of *kashrut*. They were all profoundly aware of their Jewishness, even if they were no longer clear about how to express it.

Not all of them shared the revolutionary outlook. Yet most subscribed to the secular messianism that the radicals preached: the hope for a better world. Not all of them shared the destructive anticlericalism of the anarchists and socialists, yet some immigrants happily rejected rabbinical authority and the precepts of Halakah. The elements of traditional Judaism to which they held on were those mainly that could be adapted to an ethnic rather than a religious identity. They became the consumers of a newly

developing Yiddish culture that somehow managed to preserve their sense of themselves as Jews, yet brought them in
touch with the mainstream of modern secular society.

Yiddish was the language of the immigrants. The first
Yiddish newspapers had come on the scene in New York in
the 1870s. By 1910 there were several Yiddish dailies, dozens
of weeklies, monthlies, and quarterlies, with a range from
trash to quality literature. A lively Yiddish theater came
into existence, offering at first tawdry vaudeville and cheap
melodrama, but in time talented playwrights emerged and
serious drama was performed. Yiddish poets, short-story
writers, novelists found a responsive audience as they
wrote about life in the New World and recalled the Old. In
its early days this Yiddish literature was naïve and senti-
mental, derivative and didactic, yet always radiating energy.
Shortly before the First World War it was to begin its transformation from a literature of didacticism and folkishness
to a literature of aesthetic values and profound morality,
open to all human experience, yet rooted in Jewish reality.
From its early start, Yiddish literature, theater, and journal-
ism provided the comfort of home in the alien world of the
English language. It braked the headlong flight into assimilation, yet in the long run the secular values of that Yiddish
culture eased the immigrants' accommodation to American
society.

THE *shvitser* ACCOMMODATED most rapidly to America, with
aggressive eagerness; hence he yielded up his Old World
traditions without resistance. He avidly took advantage of
America's freedom—to work at whatever he chose to do, to
educate himself and his children, to live where he pleased,
to become what he strove to be, emancipated from the social ascriptions of a stratified society and from restrictive
government laws. In 1900 nearly 20,000 East European immigrant Jews had moved from the East Side slums and were

living in Harlem, then a pleasant area settled by the German Jews after the Civil War. By 1910, about 100,000 Russian Jews lived there, and thousands of others had moved to the Bronx and Brooklyn, to Yorkville and Washington Heights. They and their children pursued education as far as it would take them. They went to school and to night school. In 1902 they filled the lecture halls of City College and some even were going to Columbia University. They were leaving the sweatshop and the factory. In the 1900 census thousands of Russian Jews and their children figured as white-collar workers and salesmen. They had already become businessmen, teachers, pharmacists, dentists, doctors, and lawyers. Many became successful through real estate. In 1901 it was said that immigrant Jews who had once lived in tenements now owned them. A few even became millionaires.

For each wave of immigration from Russia bringing penniless and green immigrants into the slums, there was an exodus by immigrants who after five or ten years or so had managed well enough so they could leave the squalor of those slums. By 1914, only about one fourth of the New York Jews lived on the Lower East Side. No other immigrant group evinced such rapid and dramatic success. Many of these Jews, in their second area of settlement, shaking off the stigma of immigrant foreignness, began then to reclaim part of the Jewish heritage they had shed.

Even the radicals and the secular Yiddishists learned to accommodate to America. It took them longer than the *shvitsers*, in part because they had created institutions embodying their original goals and values, and institutions were harder to bend than people. Abraham Cahan (1860–1951) exemplified in his life and work the gradual accommodation of doctrinaire radicalism to pragmatic socialism. He helped to shape an Americanized version of the Jewish socialism that flourished in Russia and then in Poland until

1939. In the United States, this socialism, tinged with a variant of Jewish secular ethnicism, persisted for about a half century, though in the long run it did not prove to be a viable option for Jewish continuity in America.

When Cahan came to New York from Vilna in 1882, he was already a radical. Unlike the hero of his famous novel, *The Rise of David Levinsky*, he had already shaved his beard and sidelocks, the mark of observant Jews in the Old Country, and had already discarded his prayer shawl and phylacteries. In New York Cahan began writing for the radical Yiddish press. But his talents needed a wider field and he soon began a new career as a journalist in the American press and as a novelist. When the *Jewish Daily Forward* was founded in 1897 as a Socialist daily, Cahan became its editor. But he soon left because of continuing radical factionalism within the paper and the movement. For a few years he worked under Lincoln Steffens on the *Commercial Advertiser*. In 1903 Cahan returned as editor of the *Forward*, this time on his own terms. He succeeded in transforming the paper from a dogmatic propaganda organ into a vital newspaper, responsive to its working-class immigrant readers. Though he remained a lifelong Socialist and the *Forward* remained a Socialist paper, Cahan used the *Forward* as an Americanizing instrument, to teach his readers manners, cleanliness, civics, and American history. The paper addressed itself to the family problems of immigrant life, the disintegration of the family, the rise of delinquency in the slums, and the breakdown of the traditional community. It offered its readers satisfying reading material, presented in a Yiddish style appropriate to their low cultural level, with the strong invasion of English words and largely stripped of its rich Hebrew element—the vocabulary of Talmud and tradition.

Above all, the *Forward* spoke for the workers and their economic interests not in the doctrinaire jargon of the radical parties, but in the voice of the then developing trade-union movement. For the thousands upon thousands of Jewish workers in the needle trades and other industries, their prime concern was wages and hours. As early as the 1870s Jewish tailors and capmakers had begun to form their own unions and in the 1880s had even conducted strikes for a ten-hour day and higher wages. The United Hebrew Trades, formed by socialist intellectuals in 1888, consisted at first of only three participating local unions, whose combined membership amounted to fewer than 80 persons. Two years later, the number of local unions in the UHT had risen to 22, with a membership of nearly 6,000. But in the next two decades membership in the unions constantly fluctuated.

For one thing, the early unions, organized by anarchist and socialist intellectuals, were ridden by factional radical politics that were more appropriate to party politics in Central and Eastern Europe than to the conditions in the needle trades. The union leaders occupied themselves with ideological and theoretical questions of revolutionary tactics and radical goals rather than with the bread-and-butter issues of the workers' needs. Their publications were filled with abstruse heavy material of little relevance to the workers' daily lives. Another reason for the unstable union membership was the members themselves. For most of this period, the caliber of the immigrants could be described as raw. They were rough and crude, without experience in communal life, without discipline. Their life in the Old Country had not prepared them for sustained organizational activity. The Jewish Labor Bund, eventually to become the mass labor movement and political party of the Jewish working class in czarist Russia and later in independent Poland, was founded only in 1897 in Vilna. The immigrants who came after the unsuccessful 1905 Revolution represented a new strain, for many of them had already experienced participation in a political movement.

But apart from the rawness of the early immigrants, we must reckon also with their driving ambition. That striving for success turned the newly made Jewish proletarian within one generation into a member of the middle class. To be sure, in the conditions then prevailing in America's industrial cities, these Jewish workers could not rise much above the lower middle class. But they achieved that status, becoming the shortest-lived proletarian class among any immigrant group that came to America.

The International Ladies Garment Workers Union (ILGWU), founded in 1900, had more downs than ups in the first decade of its existence. But 1910 proved to be the watershed year for Jewish trade unionism. The famous shirtwaistmakers strike—about 80 percent of 20,000 workers in this industry were young women and girls—began November 22, 1909, and lasted for twelve weeks. The strikers won improvements in their conditions, but failed to win union recognition. Some months later, in July 1910, 55,000 cloakmakers went out on strike. They were mostly Jewish workers striking against mostly Jewish employers. After seven weeks—the stumbling block in the negotiations was union recognition—prominent Jewish communal figures, with a distinguished record of service in American public life, intervened and successfully mediated an end to the strike not only in the interests of the workers and the industry, but on behalf of the larger Jewish community. The settlement, called the "Protocol of Peace," introduced a new and distinctively Jewish element in the trade-union movement, for its fundamental achievement involved the denial of the idea of class war. The Protocol underscored instead the idea of perpetual economic peace in the industry. The origins of this conciliation lay in the traditional sense of responsibility that Jews felt for each other and also in the traditional Jewish institution of *bet din*, a court of arbitration, to which Jews in conflict brought their disputes to be settled by a rabbinical judge. Traditional Jewish society had also had an institution of *borerim*, communal leaders who functioned as arbitrators and by whose decisions the involved parties agreed to abide. That pattern of conciliation and arbitration was successfully introduced into the Jewish trade-union movement and prevailed for generations, setting a model for labor peace seldom achieved in other industries.

IMMIGRATION PRODUCED upheaval and drastic change in the lives of the new arrivals. It wrought dislocation and disruption. The discontinuity between past and present, the necessary adjustment from the Old World to the New World took its toll in personal deprivation as well as communal disorder. This vast migration also had a disquieting effect on the established Jewish community and sent tremors of shock through that quarter of a million Jews who looked upon themselves as Americans and part of American society.

When the East European migration was just beginning, the American Jews and the Americanized German Jews spurned those new immigrants, because some were too Orthodox and others too radical, because some were too poor and uncouth and others too noisy and aggressive. The rising public clamor by the xenophobes, the restrictionists, and the anti-Semites against the immigrants frightened the settled Jews, who felt that their own security in America was imperiled by the newcomers. They wanted to return the immigrants to Europe. They tried to settle them in agricultural colonies or to disperse them throughout the country, as far away as possible. Nevertheless, because they shared—willingly or not—a community of fate with these

East European Jews, they undertook, however reluctantly, to help ease the strains of their new circumstances.

Though only a small proportion of the immigrants needed charity, the existing charitable organizations found themselves overwhelmed. They could not raise enough money to provide the resources to cope with destitution on a scale never before encountered in private charity. In 1883 the resources of the United Hebrew Charities of New York, then the largest relief organization, were so overtaxed that the agency protested to the European Jewish organizations and begged them to stop promoting "an indiscriminate immigration."

Yet in the next two decades the established Jews expended heroic efforts to help the immigrants settle into America. Funds were somehow raised to help the indigent. Local relief societies and fraternal orders all over the country joined the effort. In 1890 the Baron de Hirsch Fund provided an enormous sum of money to help finance the reception of the immigrants, their vocational training, and especially to encourage them to enter agricultural pursuits. The immigrants too helped themselves, through their *landsmanshaften*, self-help societies of people from the same town. They raised funds and provided an informal network of economic and moral support.

In New York, Chicago, and other cities, the American Jews undertook to educate and shape the immigrants in the image of model Americans. These American Jews were among the pioneers of a movement called "Americanization" that social workers, educators, and civic leaders soon fostered actively throughout all cities with large enclaves of foreign immigrants. The movement to Americanize the immigrants began in the 1890s and lasted well into the 1920s. It involved private agencies that operated in cooperation with local public schools and health agencies. The settlement house became the chief institution, after the public school, to help assimilate the foreigners and to turn them into American citizens. The Educational Alliance, organized in 1893 in New York's Lower East Side by the established Jewish community, the "uptown Jews," was the preeminent model of an Americanizing agency. With the cooperation of the city's Board of Education, free lectures were provided by eminent public figures on a wide range of subjects. There were classes of all sorts—in English and English literature, civics and American history, the fundamentals of personal hygiene, public sanitation, and biology. Kindergartens were set up to prepare immigrant children for public school. Evening classes were provided for working people. Even courses in vocational training were offered. Americanization was an attempt not only to wean the immigrants from their native tongues and cultures, but also to ease the travail of adjusting to a strange language and an alien culture.

The uptown Jews wanted to Americanize also the Orthodoxy of the East European immigrants. They believed that the rejection of the secular world and of secular education by the Orthodox alienated their young people who wanted to become part of American life. When the young saw no possibility of reconciliation between the Orthodox world and the modern world, they felt compelled to repudiate Orthodoxy and abandon Judaism altogether. Indeed, the established American Jews thought, immigrant radicalism and irreligion were the unfortunate but inevitable consequences of Orthodox rigidity—a conclusion that appears simplistic yet was not far from the mark when one considers the violent anticlericalism of the East European Jewish radicals.

But no alternative existed in the last decades of the nineteenth century that could appeal to the East European observant Jews. Reform Judaism was then in the ascendancy among American Jews, and to the Orthodox, Reform was anathema. Nor were they attracted to the much smaller and continually shrinking number of still traditional synagogues, some of Sephardic origin. These identified themselves with the Historical School of Judaism, which, while fully observant of Jewish law, adjusted style and language to the American scene. In 1887 a union of eleven such congregations had sponsored a Jewish Theological Seminary to train rabbis and teachers to serve American Jews, but within a decade the institution languished for lack of support.

In 1901 several prominent American Jews, themselves affiliated with Reform congregations, undertook to revive that Jewish Theological Seminary as an institution to help Americanize immigrant Orthodoxy. It was their plan that the seminary would train East European Jews to become modern English-speaking rabbis for the Orthodox immigrant community. The rabbinical training would combine modern Jewish scholarship with traditional Talmudic study. Appointed to head this seminary was Solomon Schechter, a Rumanian-born Orthodox Jew, discoverer of the Cairo Genizah, then a reader in rabbinics at Cambridge University. Schechter brought together a distinguished faculty and launched an institution that within a decade of its founding became the vital center of the rising Conservative movement. Its appeal was to those immigrants, or their children, who had already moved out of the slums into a middle-class neighborhood and who wanted to retain a Judaism appropriate to their new American status. Conservative Judaism proved to be just right for them.

Among the Orthodox themselves, a small group of young East European Jews revolted in 1912 against their parents' transplanted Orthodoxy and formed the Young Israel, eventually to become a significant force in the preservation of an Orthodoxy acculturated to modern society. It was the first step Orthodox Jews themselves took to accommodate to the realities of America.

The process of acculturation was under way in all areas of immigrant life—social, economic, political, and religious—and it continued to work also on the immigrants' children. Probably no immigrant community in America underwent so rapid a transformation from immigrants into Americans, from peddlers and proletarians into the middle class.

# II
# RESPONSIBILITY AND CRISIS, 1890–1945

# 4

# *American Jewry Comes of Age*

THE CRISES OF THE TIMES produced a new generation of leaders. The relentless persecution under which the East European Jews were languishing riveted the attention of the leading American Jews not only because those disasters affected their fellow Jews abroad, but also because of their own self-interest, because of the impact of those disasters on the American Jewish community and its own stability and security. Thus the pressures of history brought to the fore of Jewish communal life an extraordinary group of men of wealth and standing in America's most prestigious circles. These Jews, some German-born and some American-born, created a network of new institutions to carry out a wide range of functions that they had at first discharged as private individuals. The most prominent among them were the banker Jacob H. Schiff (1847–1920), the diplomat Oscar S. Straus (1850–1926), the lawyer Louis Marshall (1856–1929), and the scholar Cyrus Adler (1863–1940). All had been reared in the Jewish tradition of *zedakah*, righteousness, the performance of good deeds as a personal obligation to God, and they adhered to that tradition with spectacular generosity all their lives. They believed that their good fortune made it incumbent upon them to help the less fortunate members of their community. That traditional Jewish outlook harmonized with the venerable Protestant concept of stewardship, according to which men who benefited from God's bounty had the obligation, as stewards of that bounty, to perform good deeds and to use His bounty for social good.

The Jewish notables who assumed the responsibility of communal affairs at the end of the nineteenth century filled the vacuum of leadership that then existed. For though the Union of American Hebrew Congregations (UAHC) had been established in 1873 to be the representative spokesman for American Jews, it had never fulfilled that role. Its founder and prime mover, Isaac Mayer Wise, had instead devoted all the energies of his remaining years to Hebrew Union College and had used up the Union's resources to maintain the college. As for the Reform rabbis who had dominated the American Jewish scene, they had failed to grasp the dimensions of the East European Jewish immigration and its import for American Jewry and had defaulted on their responsibilities toward the new immigrants. The cultural differences between the Reform rabbis who had radicalized Judaism and the East European immigrants, whether they were traditionalists or atheists, had become an unbridgeable chasm.

Schiff, Straus, Marshall, Adler—together with their associates, friends, and relatives, including the Sulzbergers, the Guggenheims, the Seligmans, and countless others of that social group that became known as "our crowd"— stepped into the breach. In 1888 they established the Jewish Publication Society of America, an undertaking that Leeser had once unsuccessfully attempted. In 1891 they advised Baron Maurice de Hirsch on creating a major fund to help absorb the East European Jewish immigrants in America. In 1892 they founded the American Jewish Historical Society to record the Jewish historical presence in America from earliest times. In 1902, as we have seen, they reestablished the Jewish Theological Seminary of America.

The unhappy situation of the European Jews commanded their attention from the 1890s on, and they used all their contacts with men in high places in the government, including the President, to protest the anti-Semitic policies of European rulers. In 1902 Schiff, Straus, and Congressman Lucius N. Littauer intervened with President Theodore Roosevelt to urge the American government to express its displeasure at the Rumanian government's anti-Semitic actions. The consequence was the historic note that John Hay, then Secretary of State, addressed to the Rumanians, setting forth America's interest in Rumania's treatment of its Jews.

The pogroms in czarist Russia—the Kishenev pogrom in 1903 and the massive wave of pogroms after the 1905 Revolution—preoccupied the Jewish notables above all other concerns. They were in constant communication with Jewish leaders in England, France, and Germany. In the United States they organized massive fund-raising campaigns for the victims of the pogroms. But though their frequent intercessions with President Roosevelt and State Department officials were sympathetically received, they were unable to effect any change in the czarist government's course. When the Russo-Japanese war broke out in 1904, Schiff—through his banking firm Kuhn, Loeb and Company—and Lord Rothschild in London refused to lend Russia money. Instead they contributed a major share toward a loan of £5 million to the Japanese. (For long thereafter Jacob Schiff was a hero to the Japanese.)

Shortly after the start of the 1905 pogroms, Straus, Schiff, and Cyrus L. Sulzberger organized a National Committee for Relief of Sufferers by Russian Massacres. Within a month, eliciting the responsive support of Jews all over the country, from the established Jews to the newcomers, the committee raised over a million dollars, a level never before achieved by the local charitable agencies.

THE URGENCY of the Jewish agenda—abroad as well as at home, where the clamor against immigration was tinged with anti-Semitism—convinced Straus, Schiff, and their friends that a strong national Jewish organization was needed, comparable to the Anglo-Jewish Association in England, the Alliance Universelle Israélite in France, and the similar bodies in Germany and Austria. A national organization, authoritative and representative, would be more likely to win the confidence of even those Jewish masses whose radical commitments made them suspicious and critical of the rich and the powerful, especially when they appeared to be acting selflessly. After nearly a year of debate and deliberations, among themselves and in wider contacts throughout the American Jewish community, that Jewish elite established the American Jewish Committee (AJC), convening its first meeting on November 11, 1906. The committee's charter described its objectives:

> . . . to prevent the infraction of the civil and religious rights of the Jews, in any part of the world; to render all lawful assistance and to take appropriate remedial action in the event of threatened or actual invasion or restriction of such rights, or of unfavorable discrimination with respect thereto; to secure for Jews equality of economic, social and educational opportunity; to alleviate the consequences of persecution and to afford relief from calamities affecting Jews, wherever they may occur; and to compass these ends to administer any relief fund which shall come into its possession or

which may be received by it, in trust or otherwise, for any of the aforesaid objects or for purposes comprehended therein.

The men who formed the AJC had, by virtue of their talents and achievements, risen high in American society. That position and their dedication to the interests of the Jews validated them as leaders of the American Jewish community. Indeed, precisely such men had for centuries been elevated to places of leadership in the traditional Jewish community. The AJC elites were the modern-day counterparts of the *shtadlanim*, the Jewish elites of earlier times through whose contacts and influence with high authorities the Jewish community had sought relief and redress from oppression. But American democracy and egalitarianism had affected the outlook of many Jews in the rapidly expanding and diversifying Jewish community. Some regarded the AJC's assumption of leadership as an arrogation of power. The AJC elites, it was said, were unrepresentative of the variety of ideological strains and the multiplicity of interests among the Jews. Nor had they been given authorization to speak on behalf of the whole Jewish community.

Indeed, in 1906 the American Jewish community had become far more heterogeneous than ever before, as well as far more numerous. The first wave of East European Jewish immigrants had already become Americanized and was producing a native-born generation. But the flood of immigration still continued unabated. And the new immigrants brought with them different historic experiences from those of earlier immigrants. By 1906 the differences among the Jews in the United States were more profound than just the differences between native-born Jews and immigrants, between Jews of German origin and Jews of Russian-Polish origin, though such differences proved to be fundamental.

There was now a wide range of class and status differences among the Jews. In the openness and fluidity of America, East European immigrants and their children had already achieved status, besides financial stability. Some had emerged as political figures, elected officials, judges. Among the East European Jews and their offspring were aspirants to leadership, ready to challenge the authority of the AJC elites. Their fundamental challenge to the AJC's leadership was ideological and it embodied a confrontation between different concepts of Jewish identity, different political outlooks, and different Jewish agendas.

By 1906 three dominant views as to the nature of Jewish communal existence and the conditions for Jewish survival had emerged among the Jews in America. All these views had been shaped originally by the conditions of Jewish life in Europe and by ideas that had arisen and thrived in European Jewish society.

Schiff, Marshall, and the AJC elites articulated a view of the Jews as adherents of Judaism, bound together by the tie of religion. They repudiated the concept of Jews as a people. ("Race" was the word more frequently then in use to denote what today we call nationality, people, or ethnic group.) That definition of Jews exclusively in terms of Judaism had evolved from the time of the French Revolution and the rise of nation-state, when the Jews in France asked for political equality. In 1791 the French Revolutionary National Assembly debated whether the Ashkenazic Jews in France, who enjoyed certain rights of communal autonomy, should have the same rights of citizenship as the Sephardic Jews. The decision hinged on defining the nature of Judaism. Was it the religion of the Jews as a people, a corporate entity desiring its own autonomy, or was it the religion of individual Jews, whose observance would not prevent them from fulfilling their commitments as French citizens? The Assembly opted for the latter view, since they held that religion was a private and an individual matter. The Assembly then abolished the rights that the Jews had held as an autonomous community and voted to bestow all civic rights upon "individuals of the Jewish persuasion." The formula had been most dramatically put by Clermont-Tonnerre in the Assembly's debate on Jewish rights: "To the Jews as a nation—nothing; to the Jews as individuals—everything."

That formula became the model for Jewish identity in Western Europe and the basis on which Jews pursued political emancipation. But it was not geared to the problems in Central and Eastern Europe, where the Hapsburg and czarist empires ruled over subjects of many nationalities, who wanted not only individual rights of citizenship but also group rights, sometimes called minority rights: the right to maintain schools in their own language; cultural rights; and even political autonomy, when political independence was not attainable. In that milieu, Jews too wanted group rights—Jewish schools, Jewish institutions to be recognized and supported by the state. In that part of Europe, in that age of nationalism, Jews identified themselves as a national minority, whether they were observant Jews or secular ones. The Western model of Jewish identity by religion alone they considered to be Jewishly inadequate. They spoke pejoratively of the Western Jews as "assimilated," that is, so Westernized as to have watered down their Jewishness for acceptance in Gentile society.

In the United States, however, the channel for Jewish identity had from the start been that of a religious faith. Each American, regardless of his faith, enjoyed all civic rights. The religion he practiced was a private matter. The U.S. law never acknowledged any rights of groups, though all individuals were free to associate in groups of their own choice. All Americans had ties at one time or another to family and community in the Old Country, but they reshaped their former national ties into religious ones. American Jews too defined themselves by religion, even if they were not always religious. They explained their ties to Jews elsewhere as religious ties, though their feelings of Jewish solidarity derived from a common history and a community of fate as well as from a community of faith. That model of Jewish identity, in which Judaism was the vessel into which all the vague and inexpressible feelings of Jewish commonality were gathered, had served American Jews well until the late nineteenth century. It happened also to harmonize perfectly with the West European concept of Jewish identity that German Jews brought to America. But with the great migration from East Europe, which brought the secular national modes of Jewish identity into America, the American model of the Jews as members only of a religious faith was severely challenged.

IN 1896 THEODOR HERZL published *Der Judenstaat* ("The Jewish State") in which he proclaimed the idea of a Jewish state for the Jewish people, declaring that "we are a people—one people." A year later, the First Zionist Congress convened in Basel and gave organizational life and new impetus to the ancient Jewish longing for a return to Zion. The Zionist concept of peoplehood was a secular idea. Even though Zionism borrowed heavily from the imagery and messianic longings of Judaism, it was at bottom a secular movement that stripped Judaism from the core of Jewish national identity. Most observant Jews had indeed regarded Zionism as a heretical idea, for according to the religious tradition, the return to Zion could be fulfilled only with the coming of the Messiah. In 1902 the small number of Orthodox Jews who were Zionists founded a religious faction, called Mizrachi, within the Zionist Organization, to further the observance of Jewish law within the Zionist movement. But Zionism remained essentially a political movement and a culturally secular one. A few years after the First Zionist Congress,

Socialist-Zionist groups came into being in Russia; by 1907 they formed the World Union of the Labor Zionist movement (Poale Zion).

Zionism emerged at the time when nationalisms of all sorts were sweeping Europe, and it provided the East European Jews with a powerfully attractive option of a secular national identity. In the United States, however, as in the countries of Western Europe, the impact of Zionism was strongly negative in most quarters, though inspiring in a few. In 1898 the UAHC declared that it was "unalterably opposed to political Zionism," that though Zion was "a holy memory," America stood for their "new Zion." Schiff feared that political Zionism would place a lien on the Jews' American citizenship and endanger the relations of American Jews to their country. Louis Marshall wrote in 1901 that "the racial aspect of Judaism" did not appeal to him "as strongly as . . . the religious side."

Barely a handful of American and Americanized Jews were inspired by Herzl's vision. Some, like Stephen Wise, then a young Reform rabbi, who would years later become a great Zionist spokesman, saw in the Zionist movement "the power and pride and the nobleness of the Jewish people," in contrast to the passivity of the Jews as victims, and their pitiability as refugees. In 1898 these early American Zionists turned the motley little societies of "Lovers of Zion" into a Federation of American Zionists. The Mizrachi came on the scene in the United States in 1903, and the Poale Zion in 1905. Though the Zionists in America commanded sentiment, they were poor in numbers and organization. But their advocates were articulate and aggressive, demanding to be heard wherever Jewish communal interests were involved. They had an ideology, a systematic view of Jewish life and a solution to its anomalies, which they insisted on presenting and representing in all Jewish assemblies. These Zionists were to offer the strongest challenge to the leadership of the AJC elites and even to call into question their legitimacy as Jewish leaders. Though the Zionists lacked mass support, in terms of membership, they claimed to be more representative of the Jewish masses than the AJC elites. They clamored for democracy, charging the AJC with plutocracy and oligarchy.

Another challenge to AJC leadership came from the left, once the radicals on the East Side settled down and consolidated around the *Jewish Daily Forward*, the ILGWU, and the trade-union movement. In 1900 the Jewish Socialists formed the *Arbeter Ring*, Workmen's Circle, a fraternal society for mutual aid and the promotion of cultural activities in Yiddish. In the United States, the leaders of the Jewish socialist movement and its various factions held to the same ideas that shaped the Bund in Russia. They repudiated the idea that all Jews had common interests. Strictly hewing to the principle of class divisions and class war, they rejected collaboration with other Jewish parties or organizations, arguing that the interests of the Jewish working class were incompatible with the interests of the Jewish bourgeoisie and that Jewish workers had more in common with the working classes of other peoples. (The idea failed when it was tested in times of crisis, for when Jews were in trouble, the overpowering sense of Jewish solidarity transcended class lines.)

To be sure, there were times when the Jewish labor leaders and the Jewish socialists had to accept the mediation of the bourgeoisie, as in the establishment of the Protocol of Peace in 1910, but as a matter of principle the radicals were not prepared to join in common undertakings of the Jewish community as a whole. Nevertheless, whether it was the exigency of Jewish needs or the impact of American pragmatism, at certain occasions the Jewish socialists cooperated with other Jewish organizations. In the course of decades, as their revolutionary energy became exhausted in

72

factional politics and as the real and enormous problems of the European Jews did not permit the luxury of ideology, Jewish leftist institutions whose agenda was becoming increasingly Jewish moved closer to a consensus with the rest of the Jewish community.

THE PROBLEM of democracy in the Jewish community was to continue to disturb Jewish communal affairs for some forty years after the founding of the AJC. Among the AJC founders themselves there had been some who had advocated a democratic election of Jewish leaders by a congress of Jews. But that idea was rejected, partly because it proved unwieldy and impracticable, but more importantly because they felt that such a congress of Jews in America electing their own officials would give credence to the standing charge that the Jews constituted a state within a state. The AJC founders finally compromised by extending their base to include delegates from the B'nai B'rith and the UAHC, both organizations with pretensions to national leadership, and to provide a geographic representation also of American Jewry. Nevertheless, the right of the AJC to speak for American Jews was challenged by the Zionists, the Socialists, and the Orthodox Jews.

Within two years of the AJC's founding, New York Jews had to confront once again the thorny problem of leadership and responsibility. On September 1, 1908, New York's Police Commissioner Theodore A. Bingham charged that the Jews, then about a quarter of New York's population, accounted for half of New York's criminals. The Jewish community responded with outrage, demanding Bingham's removal. The very groups who had attacked the right of the AJC to speak for American Jews now demanded that the AJC speak on behalf of them. In the meantime, some popular leaders among the downtown Jews, responding to pressure to obtain a retraction from Bingham, called a conference of about one hundred delegates, representative of all shades of opinion among New York Jews. In one of history's little ironies, the conference concluded that influential personalities would be more effective for their purpose than a broad-based democratic body whose actions might be shaped by "unassimilated, inexperienced, and undisciplined" immigrant Jews. The downtowners had reached the same conclusions as the uptowners.

After about ten days of tumult, Marshall began confidential negotiations that extracted from Bingham a satisfactory retraction, in exchange for an end to the East Side's anti-Bingham campaign. Marshall won the concessions from the downtown Jews largely through the mediation of Judah L. Magnes, a young Reform rabbi, who enjoyed the confidence of both the uptown and downtown Jews.

The Bingham affair led to the establishment early in 1909 of the New York Kehillah as a representative body of the New York Jews. Its founding conference was attended by three hundred delegates representing 222 organizations—synagogues, charitable societies, mutual-aid societies, fraternal lodges, educational institutions, Zionist groups, and federations. The socialists, on principle, did not take part and never joined the Kehillah. The delegates approved a constitution that included a complicated arrangement whereby the Kehillah operated as a local arm of the AJC. Thus, in the interests of communal responsibility, the AJC had succeeded in exercising a measure of control over the "unruly ghetto." Magnes was elected chairman of the Kehillah and remained there until its demise in 1922.

In its short life the New York Kehillah left a record of accomplishment. It managed to contain crime and delinquency in the Jewish slums. It introduced innovative and creative programs in Jewish education. It served as a communitywide forum for the expression of a wide range of views on Jewish problems. But it failed to solve the question of representative Jewish self-government in a pluralist democracy, especially during a period of ideological differences, when consensus could be attained only on ad hoc issues.

In its early years the AJC directed its energies in the domestic field against the restriction of immigration and the imposition of literacy tests on immigrants. By dint of its diligence and the high quality of its educational campaign, the AJC managed to help keep America's gates open to the immigrants. The AJC leaders believed in the efficacy of education. Anti-Jewish attitudes were the product, they believed, of ignorance and could be dispelled by the dissemination of accurate information about the Jews and Jewish issues. The AJC took over from the Jewish Publication Society the responsibility for the *American Jewish Year Book*, which had first begun to appear in 1899.

The AJC's most spectacular success was its three-year campaign beginning in 1908 to get Congress to abrogate America's treaty with Russia because it discriminated against Jews—from any country—in the issuance of permits to enter Russia. The AJC leaders objected to America's acquiescence in Russia's discrimination against American Jews, but the passion underlying the masterful political and educational campaign was directed against Russia for its brutal pogroms and persecution of the Jews within its borders.

THE AMERICAN JEWS were sensitive to every manifestation of anti-Jewish prejudice in the United States, persevering in correcting misstatements about Jews, quick to react against social exclusion. In 1913 Marshall succeeded in having the New York State Legislature enact a civil-rights act that made it a misdemeanor for hotels or places of public accommodation to advertise any discriminatory or exclusionary practices. But America was happily free from the political anti-Semitism of Europe, where—as in Germany and Austria—political parties vied with each other in the virulence of their anti-Jewish planks, or—as in Russia—the regime fomented or encouraged anti-Jewish violence. Russia in fact exploited even the most primitive anti-Jewish superstitions, as in the case of Mendel Beilis, a Jewish watchman in Kiev, who was falsely accused, with government connivance, of killing a child to use its blood for ritual purposes. Beilis was arrested and held in prison for two years. The preposterous charge straight out of the medieval anti-Semitic repository aroused worldwide protest and denunciation. Under the eyes of the world, and defended by the best lawyers in all Russia, Beilis was finally found innocent and acquitted.

Meanwhile, in Atlanta, Georgia, on April 27, 1913, when Beilis was still awaiting trial, a murdered girl's body was found in a factory basement. A few days later, Leo Frank, a Northern Jew who was the factory's superintendent and part owner, was arrested and charged with her murder. The trial, held in August 1913, was conducted in an atmosphere of mob fury, with few of the judicial safeguards that would have ensured Frank a fair trial. Tom Watson, Georgia's most admired populist politician, a notorious demagogue and a bigot, as anti-Semitic as he was anti-Catholic, fanned local hatred of the Yankee Jew in his newspaper. Predictably the jury declared Frank guilty, though the evidence was inconclusive. He was sentenced to death. Frank's appeals to the higher courts failed, but in the summer of 1915, Georgia's governor, convinced of Frank's innocence, commuted the death sentence to life imprisonment. That commutation set off rage and prejudice not only against Frank and the "Yankee Jews" defending him, but spilled over also into boycotts and terror against the local Jews. On August 16, 1915, Frank was kidnapped from the state prison farm and lynched. His murderers, whose identities were known, were never arrested or tried. It was generally held that the real murderer was the factory's night watchman. Early in 1982, nearly seventy years later, that view was finally corroborated. Alonzo Mann, now 83 years old, then an office boy in the factory and a witness at Frank's trial, confessed that he had withheld vital evidence at the trial; that he had in fact seen the night watchman with the girl. The night watchman, he said, had threatened to kill him if he told anyone.

American Jews were deeply agitated over the Frank case because, as a disgraceful miscarriage of justice, it called in question the rule of law in America. Even more disquieting to them, however, was its revelation of the seething anti-Semitic prejudice beneath the surface of Southern society. Marshall and the AJC leaders were active behind the scenes in investigative and legal aspects of the case, but they believed that whatever was to be done "was to be done as a matter of justice," and not from a Jewish point of view. They feared that a visible "invasion" of Northern Jews in Frank's defense would intensify the prejudice of the local people. The Frank case spurred the B'nai B'rith in 1913 to establish the Anti-Defamation League, whose formation had been planned for some time as the B'nai B'rith's challenge to AJC's hegemony and to its strategy of quiet diplomacy.

The Leo Frank case was one of the ugliest anti-Semitic episodes in American history, yet it provided little insight into the nature of anti-Semitism in American society. The incident appeared to have been a sporadic eruption of violent anti-Semitism, fanned by populist agitation. It tapped dormant anti-Jewish prejudices, yet exhausted itself in one act of cruel vigilantism.

THE OUTBREAK of the First World War in August 1914 created a new and urgent agenda for American Jews. The East European Jews—the Jews who densely populated the Pale of Settlement in czarist Russia and the Jews who lived in Galicia in the Hapsburg Empire—were trapped in the eastern war zones. As the German armies advanced and retreated and as the Russian armies retreated and advanced countless times, the contending armies overran the thickly settled Jewish areas—Lemberg, Czernowitz, Warsaw, Lodz. As the front moved back and forth, the armies left in their wake ravaged Jewish communities, their shops and property plundered, their homes destroyed. Each newly invading army accused the Jews of having assisted the enemy, thus justifying further marauding and violence. (Besides the millions of Jews in the war zones, about one and a half million Jews were enlisted in their countries' military services.)

The needs of the Jews were unprecedented. America was still neutral and could provide relief. American Jewish organizations began to raise funds for the destitute East European Jews. Under AJC leadership, an American Relief Committee, uniting some thirty groups, was created to bring order out of the chaos of competitive fund raising and to ensure the collection of the huge sums needed. Meantime, the downtown Orthodox Jews and the *landsmanshaften* had formed a Central Relief Committee. The Zionists, for their part, had formed a Palestine Relief Committee, to provide the financial aid on which the Palestinian Jewish community depended and which had previously come from the East European Jews. In November 1914 these groups agreed to join the larger body formed by the AJC. The new organization was called the American Jewish Joint Distribution Committee (JDC), "joint distribution" referring to the cooperative character of the organization and its policy of equitable distribution of funds. A year later, the Jewish socialists formed the People's Relief Committee, which then joined the JDC.

JDC's first chairman was Felix Warburg, a German-born banker, a member of "our crowd," and one of AJC's elites. Under his leadership the JDC raised more than $1.5 million in 1915. By 1918 it had raised over $16 million. The JDC demonstrated, by its successful operations, that urgent Jewish concerns and nonpartisan goals could override the diverse ideological groupings within the American Jewish community. Until today the JDC has continued to elicit respect and financial support from all American Jews. Throughout Europe from the days of the First World War till after the Second, the "Joint," as European Jews called it, was associated with American generosity and the hope for Jewish survival.

THE GREAT WAR OF 1914–1918 catapulted American Jewry into world Jewish leadership, even before the war propelled the United States into the center of world politics. Besides the responsibility for the welfare of the European Jews, the American Jewish community soon assumed responsibility for their political interests as well. The most immediate obligation fell to the American Zionists. The outbreak of the war had immobilized the World Zionist Executive, whose headquarters had been in Berlin. The American Zionists stepped into the breach and set up a Provisional Executive Committee for General Zionist Affairs to continue worldwide Zionist activities. Its chairman was Louis Dembitz Brandeis (1856–1941), an American-born jurist long associated with progressive causes. In 1916 President Wilson appointed him to the U.S. Supreme Court. One of the mediators in the Protocol of Peace of 1910, Brandeis had thereafter become active in the Jewish community. He was probably the most illustrious recruit the American Zionist movement ever attracted to its ranks.

Palestine, then part of the Ottoman Empire, was ruled by the Turkish sultan, long under German influence. Once Turkey joined the Central Powers and its territory became part of the vast battlefield of the war, the disintegration of Ottoman rule in the Near East was imminent. Early in 1915, England, France, and Russia—the Allied Powers—began to lay plans for eventual postwar partition of the Ottoman Empire, and by April 1916 they had agreed on their respective spheres of influence. Palestine was to be put under international administration. The emerging territorial and political changes that offered unanticipated possibilities for establishing a Jewish state in Palestine galvanized the Zionists into action. The Zionist Provisional Executive Committee issued a call to all Jewish organizations to confer on these problems, and Brandeis himself undertook negotiations with the American Jewish Committee to ensure its necessary participation.

Meanwhile, in late August 1914, the AJC had already begun to think about the implications of the war for the East European Jews. From the start of the war, most Jews hoped for a victory by the Central Powers in order to defeat their most hated adversary, czarist Russia. The AJC addressed itself to serious consideration as to how best to obtain for the European Jews full political rights and to abolish all existing laws that discriminated against them. Consistent with its established policy of the effectiveness of quiet diplomacy, the AJC believed that public discussions of matters so sensitive would harm Jewish interests. Hence nothing came of those negotiations between the Zionists and the AJC. But the Zionists, supported by the Yiddish press, pressed to form a Jewish Congress to deal with the questions affecting Jewish postwar policies. The debate of earlier years about democracy in the Jewish community was revived. In March 1915 a Jewish Congress Organization Committee was formed, representing the Zionists and the downtown nationalist Jews. A month later Jewish Socialist and Socialist-Zionist groups formed the National Workmen's Committee for Jewish Rights. Once again American

Jews were engaged in an ideological struggle that involved not only political differences, but also strategic and tactical differences. Eventually the AJC was drawn back into negotiations on matters of substance and procedure. Both sides agreed to compromises, including one that called for the Congress to confine its purpose to securing rights for the European Jews at the peace conference and then disband. At the end of December 1916 a meeting of the joint executive committee of the new American Jewish Congress laid plans for the forthcoming election of delegates.

Momentous events, however, intervened. In March 1917 the revolutionary movement in Russia overthrew the czarist regime. A provisional constitutional government was established, one of whose first acts was the abolition of the anti-Jewish laws. The revolution converted the Jews to the Allied cause overnight. The timing was especially fortunate, because on April 6, 1917, the United States declared war on Germany. Though the elections for the American Jewish Congress were held, as planned long before, on June 10, 1917, with some 335,000 voters participating, the Congress itself was postponed until after the war, and then, postponed again until peace negotiations would begin.

Meanwhile the world's political face continued rapidly to change. In Asia, Colonel Thomas E. Lawrence launched his brilliant military maneuvers against the Turks, and Sir Edmund Allenby took over the Palestine front, beginning his advance against the Turks in October 1917. On November 2, 1917, the British government issued the Balfour Declaration, its promulgation largely the achievement of Chaim Weizmann, whose scientific services to the British during the war gave him access to Lord Balfour and a sympathetic reception for his Zionist views, and to Nahum Sokolow, a member of the Zionist Executive with extraordinary diplomatic talents. The Declaration, presented in a letter from

Lord Balfour to Lionel Walter Lord Rothschild, president of the English Zionist Federation, read:

His Majesty's Government view with favour the establishment in Palestine of a national home for the Jewish people, and will use their best endeavours to facilitate the achievement of this object, it being clearly understood that nothing shall be done which may prejudice the civil and religious rights of existing non-Jewish communities in Palestine, or the rights and political status enjoyed by Jews in any other country.

Before the Jews could assess the Declaration's impact in transforming messianic visions into political realities, another historic convulsion overtook the Jews. On November 7, 1917, the Bolsheviks seized power in Russia. Their coup had been facilitated by the calculating connivance of the German High Command in returning Lenin to Russia in a sealed train earlier that year. For the Germans expected—correctly—that once in power, the Bolsheviks would withdraw from the war. But the Bolshevik takeover spawned a bloody civil war in Russia that lasted until 1921. That war between the Reds and the Whites played itself out in an endless series of pogroms in the Ukraine and in Poland, where the Jews were plundered, tortured, and massacred.

The political reverberations set off by the Balfour Declaration and the Bolshevik Revolution persisted for many decades. Even today they resonate throughout the world. Both events created shock waves in the American Jewish community and for about three decades American Jews were bitterly divided over both. The Balfour Declaration divided the American Jews into three factions: Zionists, anti-Zionists, and those who called themselves "non-Zionists." The non-Zionists were willing to help in the upbuilding of Palestine as a place of refuge for persecuted

Jews, but they balked at the concept of Palestine as a "national home for the Jewish people," believing that Jews were at home wherever they were accepted as equal citizens. The Bolshevik Revolution, for its part, divided the Jewish socialists, as it divided the worldwide socialist movement. In the next decade, nearly every Jewish socialist organization and labor union split into Socialist, Communist, and sometimes Trotskyite factions. In that struggle, the Jewish labor movement, built with the vision of the Jewish socialists for a better world, was nearly destroyed by their Communist offshoots, who perverted that dream.

ON DECEMBER 18, 1918, a month after the Great War ended, the American Jewish Congress met in Philadelphia and elected as its president Judge Julian W. Mack of Chicago, who had succeeded Brandeis as head of the Federation of American Zionists. Louis Marshall was elected one of the vice-presidents. Meanwhile, the American Jewish Committee, the Zionists in the United States and abroad, and the Jewish organizations of Western Europe had given much thought to the question of rights for the East European Jews. The Americans, the Zionists, and the spokesmen of the East European Jews had reached a compromise position on their advocacy of national rights and established an overall Committee of Jewish Delegations, which was to lobby on behalf of Jewish rights with the Allied delegations to the Paris Peace Conference. The French and English Jewish organizations, opposing national rights for fear that such advocacy might prejudice their own position in their own countries, contented themselves with advocacy of individual political and religious rights. The World Zionist Organization took over the responsibility to present the Jewish case for Palestine.

The tact and diplomacy employed by Louis Marshall and Cyrus Adler in formulating a common platform upon

which the differing groups could agree served substantive
goals. They finally settled on a formula not of "national"
rights, but of "racial, religious, or linguistic" rights. The
Jewish delegates' success was due first of all to the patient,
conscientious, and carefully prepared presentations that
Mack, Marshall, and Adler made to the American peace
commissioners and secondly to their long-standing friend-
ships and contacts with the American political leaders then
in high places in the government and at the peace conference. That success represented a triumph of moderation
over intemperance, of strategy over ideology. The Jewish
delegates obtained guarantees for all minorities—not just
the Jews—in the states that would be newly formed. Each
new state was obligated to:

> embody in a treaty with the principal Allied and Asso-
> ciated Powers such provisions as may be deemed nec-
> essary by the said powers to protect the interests of
> inhabitants of that State who differ from the majority
> of the population in race, language or religion. [The
> detailed provisions stipulated in each of the treaties] so
> far as they affect persons belonging to racial, religious,
> or linguistic minorities constitute obligations of inter-
> national concern and shall be placed under the guaran-
> tee of the League of Nations.

The treaties with Poland, Rumania, Austria, Hungary,
Czechoslovakia, Yugoslavia, Bulgaria, and Greece all con-
tained such provisions; later on, the Baltic countries (Lithuania, Latvia, Estonia, and Finland), whose independence
was established after the treaty of Brest-Litovsk, had to
pledge to respect the rights of minorities in order to be
admitted to the League of Nations.

Thus a state's legitimacy was made to rest on its obligation to respect the rights of minorities. The obligation

was not only national, but international, subject to enforcement by the newly formed League of Nations. The Jewish delegation to the peace conference had contributed a notable achievement to the development of international law.

Europe stood at the threshold of a new era. The old despotisms had come to an end. Subjugated peoples had attained their independence. Constitutional government had become the order of the day. Yet within a decade that bright promise of constitutionality and respect for rights— of majorities as well as of minorities—disappeared from most of Europe. The hope for a society based on law gave way to despair as lawlessness and violence escalated.

# 5

## *Decades of Anxiety,*
## *1920–1939*

THE UNITED STATES had entered the Great War in 1917 with the purpose, as President Woodrow Wilson had put it, of making the world safe for democracy. American help insured the Allies' victory in that war. The Armistice and the peace treaties were formulated and concluded on the basis of Wilson's Fourteen Points, his idealistic proposal for a postwar peace program, whose final point envisaged the establishment of the League of Nations. It was a dream of world peace and international law. At the war's end Wilson and the Americans were esteemed and acclaimed all over Europe. Yet precisely then the United States turned away from Europe and repudiated its role in world leadership. The Senate rejected America's participation in the League of Nations. The internationalists in American politics gave way to the isolationists, the progressives to the conservatives. The xenophobes came to the surface of American politics.

The Bolshevik takeover in Russia, the abortive Communist coup in Germany, and Bela Kun's short-lived Communist regime in Hungary agitated the Americans, whose suspicion and fear of alien radicals had already become widespread in the last decades of the nineteenth century. The Bolsheviks' actual seizure of power had galvanized American conservatives and isolationists into a frenzy of antiradical propaganda and action. A. Mitchell Palmer, the U.S. Attorney General (1919–1921), authorized raids to round up allegedly subversive aliens for deportation. The notorious sweeps netted about three thousand radicals, though only a few hundred were ever actually deported from the United States. In the concomitant antiradical propaganda, the canard against the "Jew-Bolshevik" appeared with increasing frequency. Among those arrested were a few Jews.

Other disquieting xenophobic trends had originated just before America's entry into the war. In November 1915 the Ku Klux Klan came to life again, to wage war not only against Negroes but also against Catholics, Jews, and foreigners, and to defend fundamentalist beliefs. In the early 1920s the Klan was reputed to have signed up about five million members in the North, South, and Midwest. Some of its members held high political offices in several states. But in 1923 the first exposés of Klan terror and violence began to appear in the national press, heralding the Klan's decline. After a top Klan leader was convicted of murder in Vincennes, Indiana, in 1925, Klan membership dropped rapidly and by 1930 it was estimated to be about nine thousand in all the United States.

The xenophobes' most enduring achievement was the enactment, first in 1921 and then in 1924 in a more stringent form, of a rigid quota law restricting immigration. Since mass immigration had begun, American nativists, influenced by racialist ideas imported from France and Germany, advocated that immigration into the United States be limited to "Nordics," that is, to people from those countries that had provided the Old Immigration. In 1908 William Z. Ripley, who had some years earlier published a learned tome, *The Races of Europe,* introduced the American public to notions derived from Mendelian genetics, to the effect that hybridization of races produced the reversion to a primitive type. This pseudoscientific racism became a passionate crusade of Madison Grant, a naturalist of a patrician family, who hated all foreigners and Jews most venomously. His most influential book, *The Passing of the Great Race,* published in 1916, argued that the immigration of "undesirable" racial groups would encourage racial blending that in turn would produce racial degeneration and bring about the suicide of desirable racial groups. "The cross between any of the three European races and a Jew," he wrote, "is a Jew."

Immigration from Europe had declined drastically during the war, and the Red scare of the Palmer Raids after the war had sparked an exodus of foreigners. But soon the flow of immigration resumed. In 1919 and 1920 the pogroms during Russia's civil war and in New Poland drove some 119,000 Jews to America's shores. The renewed immigration intensified the anti-immigration agitation. The campaign to legislate restriction was propelled with great energy by a congressman who had been profoundly influenced by Madison Grant's ideas. The law, as eventually enacted, enshrined the notion of the "racial Nordic" character of America's population and used a quota of national origins to preserve that character. The law, signed by President Calvin Coolidge on May 26, 1924, despite the great pressure for his veto, altogether prohibited Japanese immigration and permitted for the next three years only about 287,000 immigrants to enter annually, at a rate of no more than 2 percent of the foreign-born of each nationality in the United States according to the 1890 census. Thereafter, European immigrants would be still further limited—to

150,000 a year—in accordance with a fixed ratio of national origins in the white population of 1920 and with fixed quotas set for individual countries. The Immigration Act of 1924, whose national-origins clause went into effect in 1929, ended the era of unrestricted immigration in the United States. It marked the nativists' great victory and would soon cast a darkening shadow. No one knew then, but that law would later spell death and destruction for hundreds of thousands of European Jews who tried to flee Europe when flight was still possible.

Anti-Semitism was one of the durable and essential elements of American xenophobia, but the anti-Jewish thrust of the KKK and the immigration restrictions tended to become somewhat blunted because of the wide-ranging and indiscriminate hatred that the xenophobes directed against Catholics as well as Jews, against all foreigners and all radicals. The ugly and virulent hatred of foreigners and radicals was epitomized in the Sacco-Vanzetti case. In 1920 two Italian anarchists were arrested, charged with the murder of a paymaster at a shoe factory in South Braintree, Massachusetts. They were convicted in 1921. Despite the insubstantial evidence and the prejudicial atmosphere, despite nationwide and worldwide protests and despite judicial review, they were executed in 1927. The case, an international cause célèbre, represented American xenophobia at its ugliest.

In precisely the same time span of the Sacco-Vanzetti case, the American Jews became the target of an unprecedented anti-Semitic propaganda campaign conducted by Henry Ford, the man who had produced the first "Model T" automobile. Known for his advocacy of idiosyncratic ideas, Ford turned anti-Jewish, probably under the influence of German racists and White Russian anti-Semites. In 1919 he bought a weekly newspaper, the *Dearborn Independent*, and dedicated it to the publication of what he described as the "neglected truth." In May 1920 the *Independent* began publishing a series of lurid articles entitled "The International Jew." At first written by the paper's editor, the articles were a potpourri of anti-Semitic trash culled from many sources and current controversies; but the editor was soon furnished with the *Protocols of the Elders of Zion*, that notorious anti-Semitic forgery concocted by the czarist secret police around the turn of the century, which claimed that a cabal of Jewish elders ruled the world. The *Protocols* reached the West after the Russian Revolution, when the Black Hundreds—members of virulent anti-Semitic groups that fomented pogroms—fled Russia with the departing German armies and took along their anti-Semitic propaganda. The *Protocols*, when first published in German in 1920, made a great impact on Adolf Hitler.

Their impact on Henry Ford was not inconsiderable. Ford's republication of the *Protocols* in the *Dearborn Independent* catapulted him into national notoriety. He compelled Ford auto dealers and agents to subscribe to the paper and he also distributed hundreds of thousands of copies free throughout the country. After the series was completed, Ford issued them in a book entitled *The International Jew: the world's foremost problem*, which in turn was translated into German, Russian, and Spanish. These editions were distributed widely throughout the world. In the United States alone half a million copies were in circulation.

Outrage and protest greeted Ford's mass slander of the Jews. Jewish organizations, spearheaded by the American Jewish Committee, launched a countercampaign, vigorously supported by the Federal Council of the Churches of Christ in America. Over 110 of America's most distinguished leaders, including Presidents Wilson and Taft, issued a sharp protest against Ford's "vicious propaganda." In 1921 *The History of a Lie*, an account of how the *Protocols* were forged, was published by Herman Bernstein, a Jewish journalist.

For several years Ford continued to issue his anti-Semitic publications. Finally, under pressure of several law-suits and the force of public opinion, Ford agreed to call a halt to his anti-Semitic propaganda and to retract the terrible charges he had made against the Jews. Negotiations were concluded with the American Jewish Committee, and Ford's statement of apology was drafted by Louis Marshall himself. Dated June 30, 1927, Ford declared that he was "deeply mortified" that his paper had given currency to the *Protocols*, writings that had been demonstrated to be forgeries. He further expressed his awareness "of the virtues of the Jewish people as a whole, of what they and their ancestors have done for civilization and for mankind and toward the development of commerce and industry, of their sobriety and diligence, their benevolence and their unselfish interest in the public welfare."

The *Dearborn Independent* ceased publication at the end of 1927. Ford, still prodded by the Jewish leaders, ordered the destruction of thousands of copies of *The International Jew*. Yet that book of ugly anti-Semitic lies that he had fathered continued to circulate in countries where it reinforced ancient anti-Semitic prejudices. In the United States Ford's publications, elaborating on earlier nativist propaganda, lent to homegrown anti-Semites the authority of Ford's name and position and helped to nurture the marginal anti-Semitic groups that soon began to mushroom throughout the country.

Among America's patricians and Brahmins, anti-Jewish prejudice had first expressed itself in the exclusivism of their social snobbery and in their fastidious recoil from the foreignness of the Jewish immigrants and from the vulgarity of the nouveaux riches. Later it found its outlet in the exclusionary movement of the immigration restrictionists, which after the war turned to another form of anti-Jewish exclusivism—limiting Jewish enrollments in America's elite universities.

Since the turn of the century, Jews—native-born and even immigrant—had been entering American colleges and universities in large numbers in pursuit of higher education and professional careers. By 1920 New York's City College and Hunter College, both free schools, were estimated to have Jewish enrollments amounting to 80 to 90 percent of the whole student body. Before the First World War, Columbia University's enrollment was about 40 percent Jewish and Harvard's 20 percent. The period was one, to be sure, of unparalleled growth in higher education in the United States in both the number of institutions and their student enrollments.

In 1906 the Jewish presence at Harvard was sufficiently evident for some twenty or so Jewish students to form the Harvard Menorah Society, whose purpose was to obtain academic recognition for Jewish studies and, perhaps more important, to help raise the self-esteem of the Jewish students in the face of Harvard's genteel anti-Semitism, even under the then liberal administration of Harvard's President Charles W. Eliot. The Menorah Society hoped also to bridge the social and cultural gulf between the German and Russian Jewish students then attending Harvard. By 1913 similar groups had been formed at eleven other campuses to establish the Intercollegiate Menorah Association.

After the war, some Eastern colleges, no doubt affected by the xenophobic nationalism and anti-Jewish sentiment in the country, and also experiencing a shift in educational goals, began to seek ways to reduce Jewish enrollment. Discreetly, surreptitiously, they instituted a quota system limiting the number of Jewish students. Within a decade Jewish enrollment at Harvard, Columbia, New York University, and other schools dropped sharply. Hundreds of

Jewish students who had wished to attend these elite colleges were turned away. Nevertheless, at the same time, tens of thousands of Jews—immigrants, and children and grandchildren of immigrants—availed themselves of free higher education in the great cities in which they lived.

It is a paradox of Jewish history that the anti-Semitism propagated in the United States after the First World War wrought more damage to the European Jews than to the American Jews. The restriction of immigration in accordance with the national-origins quota prevented hundreds of thousands of Jews from entering America in years to come when the difference was a difference between life and death. Henry Ford's propaganda, however offensive and distressing, had no discernible or measurable impact on the status of the Jews in the United States: no violence was committed against them; they were not deprived of their civic rights; the government instituted no discrimination against them. But in Central Europe Ford's propaganda nourished the already rabid racist anti-Semitism that found its ultimate expression in German National Socialism.

For the Jews, America was indeed different. The difference grew more visible and more profound in the next three decades. Though the American Jewish Committee was constantly preoccupied with Henry Ford, the Ku Klux Klan, immigration restriction, Ivy League quotas, its overarching preoccupations were the persecutions of the Jews in Europe. The Bolshevik seizure of power and the rise of dictatorial rule under Lenin cut the Russian Jews off from normal contacts with Jews abroad. (The AJC elites, as individuals, tried to support Russian groups that hoped to bring constitutional democratic government to Russia.) In the Soviet Union in the 1920s the Jewish community and its institutions, both traditional and secular, as they had existed before the revolution and continued to exist in Poland, the Baltic countries, Rumania, and Hungary, were being wiped

out, though some tried to maintain an underground existence. The whole structure of observant Judaism was dis-
mantled. Modern secular Jewish movements—Zionism,
Jewish socialism—were declared counterrevolutionary and
proscribed. The use of Hebrew was outlawed, though Jewish schools using Yiddish as the language of instruction
were permitted for a while, but only because their curricula
conformed to Bolshevik standards and not to Jewish cultural traditions.

In Poland, Rumania, and Hungary, the governments
continued to discriminate against the Jews, limiting their
opportunities for a livelihood, restricting their access to
higher education, disseminating anti-Semitic propaganda.
In Rumania there were violent anti-Jewish outbreaks. In
Germany, under the Weimar Republic, the Jews for the first
time in their history enjoyed full political and civic equality. Nevertheless, just as the Weimar Republic itself was
under assault from Germany's nationalist right, so the Jews
were the target of vicious anti-Semitic propaganda that em-
anated from Germany's nationalist rightist political parties,
including the new upstart National Socialist German Workers' Party. The American Jewish Committee actively sought
to meet with representatives of these countries, hoping by
their efforts to alleviate the situation of the Jews. As best
they could, they tried to engage American government officials and diplomats in support of their intercessions. But
the promise of the peace after the war never materialized.
Anti-Semitism in Europe seemed to be advancing inexora-
bly, despite the guarantees of Jewish rights, despite inter-
ventions and protests.

AMERICAN JEWS, meanwhile, benefitting from the decade of
postwar prosperity, continued their upward passage into
the middle class. Always an urban people, the Jews concentrated in America's big cities. In 1900 about two thirds of all

American Jews had lived in New York, Chicago, Philadelphia, Boston, St. Louis, and Baltimore. Thirty years later, Cleveland, Detroit, and Los Angeles had overtaken Baltimore and St. Louis as cities with the largest Jewish populations. The westward movement had already begun. Within the big cities, most Jews had by the early 1930s moved from the old immigrant neighborhoods and spread throughout the cities into newer neighborhoods of a middle-class character. The increasingly middle-class character of American Jews was evident also in their rapidly falling birthrate.

By late 1929, just before the stock market crashed, a large segment of East European Jews—mostly the children of immigrants—had already made the transition from working-class status to white-collar jobholding and professional rank. Jews played a dominant and innovative role in trade and commerce of every sort. In manufacturing they clustered in the clothing trades and the food industry. They moved into real-estate brokerage, building contracting, and the junk business. They created the motion-picture industry and played a major role in the entertainment world. By the late 1920s many East European Jews could afford to give their children the same advantages in the pursuit of higher education and career that the German Jews had given *their* children a half century earlier.

The Great Depression halted Jewish mobility, but it did not impede the Jews in their pursuit of higher education. Because so many Jews were self-employed, they seemed to weather the economic hardships better than those masses of Americans employed in America's basic industries. The scarcity of capital turned many Jews from business to civil-service employment. Jews entered the city, state, and federal government bureaucracies in large numbers, as clerks, secretaries, administrators, and professionals. They became teachers in the big-city public schools.

Politics too began to attract Jews. Ambitious young

lawyers turned to elective politics to make their careers, and by the early 1930s Jews in Congress—not to speak of city councilmen in the big urban centers and state legislators—were a common phenomenon. The three Jewish governors then included New York's Herbert H. Lehman, son of a Jewish immigrant from Bavaria, who had built a small business into a major investment bank.

Since 1928, when Al Smith ran unsuccessfully as the Democratic candidate for President, American Jews identified with the Democratic Party both as voters and as candidates for political office. That loyalty was reinforced by the Jews' adoration of Franklin Delano Roosevelt for his liberalism, for the hope he gave of a world of justice and equality. Furthermore, during the Roosevelt presidency Jews entered the service of the federal government in significant numbers at the highest levels, as presidential advisers and in other high-ranking positions.

The 1920s were a time of social and moral restlessness. America had become an urban nation and its values were no longer defined by the old-fashioned religion. In fact, a religious depression preceded the economic depression in the United States. Church attendance all over America declined; the major church foreign missions failed to attract young people or sufficient financial support. The dominant Protestant churches, having identified the American pursuit of business with religion, lost much of their moral authority. Meanwhile, the Fundamentalists, who a decade earlier had succeeded in enacting the Prohibition amendment, became a national laughingstock in 1925 with the "monkey trial," when John Scopes, a Tennessee school teacher, was tried for teaching the theory of evolution. In the years that followed, many Americans expressed their religious and moral impulses in the secular protest movements, while the churches' social-action movement tried to hold on to their declining membership by confronting contemporary social issues.

THE DEPRESSION spurred liberal political thought and action among American intellectuals and activists. As hunger and distress spread across America, more and more Americans focused their attention on social and economic questions while regarding religion—its observance and values—as irrelevant to the needs of the time. Roosevelt's election and the inauguration of the New Deal in 1933 dramatized America's turn toward social and economic reform. It was a time when Americans became more responsive to European ideologies and when socialist and Communist ideas, imported from Europe, penetrated into American liberal and radical thought.

The secularist mood in America and the movement toward social concerns synchronized with the moods and trends then dominant among American Jews. Except for pockets of observant Jews, except for pockets of committed Yiddishists, except for pockets of Zionists, the mass of Jewish immigrants, and especially their American-born children, looked upon Jewishness and Judaism as liabilities, stigmata of foreignness, impediments to becoming fully American, accepted, and financially or intellectually successful. Most European immigrants, in becoming Americanized, relinquished the language of their old home but, as the U.S. Census showed, few groups discarded their language as rapidly as the East European Jews abandoned Yiddish. Furthermore, at least three fourths of Jewish parents neglected to give their children any Jewish education or to transmit any knowledge of Judaism.

The story of how the B'nai B'rith Hillel Foundation came into being is dramatic evidence of the low estate of Jewish learning and literacy then. In the early 1920s about two hundred Jewish students were enrolled at the University of Illinois at Urbana, a few dozen of whom belonged to the Intercollegiate Menorah Association. Some of these Jewish students took a course in biblical literature given by Edward Chauncey Baldwin, a noted Bible scholar and a practicing Christian. Astonished and grieved to discover that his Jewish students knew little, if anything, of their Bible, he urged Jewish rabbinic and lay leaders to take steps to remedy the situation. Finally, in 1923, Benjamin M. Frankel, a student rabbi from Hebrew Union College, who as a circuit rider served small outlying communities, took up Professor Baldwin's challenge. His energy and commitment led to the establishment of the Hillel Foundation at Urbana, modeled on the Methodist Wesley Foundation there. Its objective was to counteract the indifference of young Jews to their own religious tradition and culture. In the decades ahead the Hillel Foundation formed chapters at scores of university campuses in the United States.

Jewish education at the elementary level in the 1920s and 1930s was in a sorry state. A survey of the status of Jewish school enrollment in Cleveland in 1936 lamented prevailing conditions:

The general decline of religion, the desire and necessity of conforming; the multitudinous and harassing attractions of modern life; the state's priority on the child's time for public school; the encroachment of other agencies on the leisure of the child—these and many other features of the modern American scene are undermining the attendance of the traditional intensive Jewish school.

Indifference to Judaism was widespread among Jews. Surveys conducted in the 1930s among Americans of all faiths showed a universal decline in religious beliefs and attendance at religious services, but the decline was most marked among young Jews. In comparison with Protestants and Catholics, they disbelieved more in traditional religion, declaring themselves atheists or agnostics. A study made in New York in 1935 found that three fourths of young Jews had not attended any religious services at all during the past year.

Though only a third of all Jews were affiliated with a synagogue, the number of congregations being formed and synagogues being built continued to increase in the 1920s and 1930s. New institutions of religious life came into being among Orthodox and non-Orthodox groups. All, whatever their particular function and their general outlook, were committed to strengthening the ties of American Jews to Judaism, to act as a bulwark against the powerful forces of assimilation in America. Yet all these institutions were themselves products of the new kind of Jewish life that was taking shape in America. The Orthodox institutions—like Yeshiva College, established in 1928 as an outgrowth of Rabbi Isaac Elchanon Theological Seminary (RIETS), founded in 1897—represented an Orthodox compromise with America and with modernity. For the world of Orthodox Jewry, in America as in Eastern Europe, was only then coming to terms with the modern secular world slowly and reluctantly by accepting secular education as part of a young Jew's necessary intellectual training. The Rabbinical Council of America and the expansion of the Young Israel into a national institution bespoke the growing presence of Orthodox rabbis with American experience and an American outlook.

To attract and hold their members, the Reform and Conservative synagogues embraced secular Jewish functions, serving as community centers, providing facilities for the host of philanthropic, Zionist, nationalist, and cultural activities that then commanded the loyalties of the Jews.

The synagogue tried to become a "Jewish center," a concept first developed by Mordecai M. Kaplan (born 1881), who had been ordained at the Jewish Theological Seminary, served as a rabbi in an Orthodox synagogue, and taught at the Seminary. Kaplan conceived of the synagogue as a central communal institution in which worship, study, and fellowship could be integrated. In 1934 Kaplan expanded and developed his ideas into an overarching philosophy set forth in his book *Judaism as a Civilization*. This philosophy became the ideology for Kaplan's Reconstructionist movement, whose adherents were regarded as a left wing of Conservative Judaism. In his efforts to halt secularism's disintegrating impact upon traditional Judaism, Kaplan undertook to reinterpret Judaism not as a religion only, but as a continually evolving religious civilization whose constituent elements included religion, peoplehood, community, culture, and ethics. Kaplan's Judaism was naturalist and humanist, not a religion of revelation. To him Judaism was an expression of Jewish collective national identity, with Zionism and Palestine occupying a central place in his concept of Judaism as a civilization. Though he had ceased to advocate the observance of Jewish law as divinely commanded and obligatory, he held that "rituals" were necessary to the extent that they served the ends of group survival and personal self-fulfillment of the Jews. Kaplan continued to teach at the Seminary, though Conservatives and especially Orthodox Jews violently disagreed with his views. Nevertheless, he probably succeeded more than any other Jewish thinker in attracting young men to the service of the Jewish community at a time when the rabbinate had lost its appeal and when traditional Jewish learning did not elicit great esteem or rewards in the Jewish community.

While Kaplan was attempting to "reform" the Conservative movement, moving it away from traditionalism, the Reform rabbis began to turn, however slightly, toward tradition. In 1935 the Central Conference of American Rabbis adopted a neutral, rather than a hostile, position on Zionism, and in 1937, at a meeting in Columbus, Ohio, the Reform rabbis adopted the so-called Columbus Platform, superseding the Pittsburgh Platform of 1885. The Columbus Platform took a more conciliatory approach toward Hebrew, traditional Jewish law, and Zionism.

Despite the xenophobia and anti-Semitism of the 1920s, American Jews continued to root themselves in America not only socioeconomically but also culturally. By the late 1920s, Jewish writers—Ludwig Lewisohn, Edna Ferber, Waldo D. Frank, Elmer Rice, for instance—were a felt presence in American literature. In the next decades Jews and Jewish themes began to appear with increasing frequency in American fiction and poetry, in American drama, and in American painting.

THE 1930s INTRODUCED a new agenda into American life, one whose priorities were determined by the impact of the Depression and the thrust toward social and economic reform, and also by European developments. On January 30, 1933, Hitler and his National Socialist party came to power in Germany, introducing terror, violence, and racist anti-Semitism as the means of governance.

The situation of the Jews in Germany changed drastically in early April 1933, as the first anti-Jewish legislation was enacted and Jews were barred from all forms of government service. In 1935 the Nuremberg Laws were enacted, separating the Jews socially and racially from the rest of the German population. This racist legislation eventually determined who would live and who would die in the Third Reich and in the territories it occupied during the war.

Hitler's success at home and his successful challenges to the West in foreign affairs encouraged fascist parties and movements elsewhere in Europe—in Rumania, Hungary,

Poland, the Baltic countries. Everywhere the situation of the Jews deteriorated. Everywhere the Jews became unwanted, hounded, persecuted. There were few wide-open gates for refugees, especially Jewish ones. Immigration even to Palestine became restricted. After Arab violence against Jewish settlers in Palestine in 1929, the British began to restrict Jewish immigration. But under the pressure of the Nazi peril, the British allowed greater numbers of European Jews to enter Palestine. The Arabs responded with violence and guerrilla attacks against the Jews. In May 1939, the British issued a White Paper, drastically restricting Jewish immigration and settlement in Palestine.

Within the narrow limits of the rigid immigration laws, America admitted several thousand refugees from Germany, probably the most intellectual and creative migrants ever to enter America, the most famous among them Albert Einstein. They transformed the scientific, artistic, scholarly, and cultural face of America in the course of the next two decades—in physics, biology, psychoanalysis, sociology, economics, music, art, and literature. But these were among the fortunate few who were able to flee.

Xenophobia in the United States intensified, exacerbated by the Depression. Unceasing efforts by Jewish organizations to have Congress enact immigration legislation of an emergency character repeatedly failed. America's deep-rooted nativist prejudices were reinforced by the spread of Nazism in Europe, as pro-Nazi, anti-Semitic groups mushroomed in the United States. The German-American Bund served as a propaganda conduit between the European Nazis and America's homegrown anti-Semites. Charles E. Coughlin, a Catholic priest, became America's most virulent anti-Semite, spouting his vicious propaganda in nationwide weekly radio broadcasts and in a periodical, *Social Justice*, whose early issues reprinted the *Protocols of the Elders of Zion*. Yet, extraordinarily, there is no evidence that American Jews suffered significant discrimination or liabilities as a consequence of the Depression or the rise of Nazi-inspired anti-Semitism. Once again, as in the past, the victims of American anti-Semitism were the European Jews, for whom no place could be made in the United States, apart from the narrowly prescribed limits of the immigration laws. In July 1938 President Roosevelt called an international conference on the refugee problem in Evian, France. Though small practical gains were achieved, the great expectations for which Jews had hoped were not realized.

Having annexed Austria in March 1938, Hitler continued to threaten the peace of Europe, and the Third Reich continued on its inexorable anti-Jewish course. The assassination of a minor German diplomat in Paris by a young Jewish refugee early in November set off the fearful *Kristallnacht* of November 9–10, 1938. All over Germany synagogues and other Jewish institutions went up in flames. The tide of Jewish refugees swelled.

In their panic to flee Europe, to get the precious documents that would gain them sanctuary somewhere, Jews grasped at any papers and permits. Some were faked and some, though genuine, were later invalidated by the same government that had issued them. The most tragic case was the boatload of 936 Jewish refugees from Germany who arrived in Cuba on the *St. Louis* in May 1939 only to be refused admission on the grounds that their entry permits were invalid. Through the heroic efforts of the Joint Distribution Committee, the unfortunate Jews were finally admitted to England, Belgium, Holland, and France.

As the decade of the 1930s came to an end, Jews in America had clearly become the most fortunate Jews in the world. They had weathered two decades of anxiety. They had experienced repeated barrages of anti-Semitic propaganda and an economic depression. Though many of America's social, educational, and cultural institutions of high status had raised barriers against them, the Jews had attained distinction in many fields.

But American Jews lacked political power and political leverage. A mere 3 percent of America's population, they could not transform America's xenophobic, isolationist, inward-looking character, even though they had access to men in high political office, including President Roosevelt. It was perhaps unrealistic of them to have hoped to turn America around, but that had been their hope against hope.

# 6

# The Great Ordeal

On January 30, 1939, Adolf Hitler addressed the Reichstag on the sixth anniversary of his accession to power. Once again he threatened Europe with war and, even more ominously, warned that he would then destroy the European Jews. In mid-March 1939, defying the British and French, and with accelerating aggressiveness, Hitler annexed Czechoslovakia's western provinces and made a puppet state out of Slovakia, its eastern province. While planning his next depredation, the conquest of Poland, Hitler seized an unforeseen and improbable opportunity for a rapprochement with the Soviet Union, his most abominated enemy after the Jews. The secret negotiations between the two totalitarian dictatorships coincided with Hitler's intensifying provocations against Poland. On August 24, 1939, the announcement of a nonaggression pact between Hitler's Germany and Stalin's Russia shocked and dismayed the world.

Having signed also a secret protocol that divided Poland between Germany and the Soviet Union, and thus secure on his eastern flank, Hitler invaded Poland on September 1, 1939. Two days later, England and France, honoring their guarantees to aid Poland, declared war on Germany. The Second World War had begun. By the end of September, Poland had fallen, partitioned between Germany and the Soviet Union. In Poland the SS began immediately to carry out the preliminary stages of Hitler's long-range plan to destroy the European Jews, whose code name was the Final Solution.

Hitler then prepared to invade Western Europe. While the SS was incarcerating the Polish Jews in ghettos, the Third Reich's armed forces invaded Denmark and Norway in April 1940 and in May overran the Netherlands, Belgium, and France. After the French surrendered on June 21, 1940, Hitler stood at the English Channel, ready to launch an invasion of Britain once he attained his anticipated air supremacy.

As Europe hurtled toward havoc and death, the United States remained neutral. Its neutrality was a heritage of America's isolationist reaction after the First World War. Still, Americans anxiously observed Hitler's rise to power, his policy of remilitarization in violation of his nation's international obligations. Americans watched Mussolini's invasion and annexation of Ethiopia and then stood by while General Francisco Franco, supported by Nazi Germany and Fascist Italy, overthrew the Spanish Republic in 1936. Americans looked on while Japan invaded China in 1937. All these aggressions confirmed Americans in their fears of foreign involvements and prompted Congress to enact neutrality laws designed to maintain an embargo on American munitions and loans to belligerents and to keep Americans out of any involvement with them.

BUT THE MOOD in the United States gradually began to shift after Germany invaded Poland and once England and

France had declared war on Germany. Roosevelt himself began to pursue a more active policy of countering congressional isolationism and started to move the United States from a position of neutrality to nonbelligerency. In November 1939 Congress amended an earlier Neutrality Act to permit the sale of arms to belligerents on a cash-and-carry basis. In the summer of 1940, when England stood alone against the Nazi fury, Roosevelt, in response to Winston Churchill, Britain's new Prime Minister, arranged an "exchange" of American destroyers for British naval bases in the Caribbean, thus managing to come to England's aid while circumventing the neutrality laws and the persistent isolationist prejudices in the United States. In September 1940 Congress approved the Selective Training and Service Act, the first peacetime military draft in the United States. Later that month Japan signed a military and economic pact with Germany and Italy to form the Berlin-Rome-Tokyo Axis, in effect combining the conflicts in Europe and Asia into what would soon become one global war.

Meantime a presidential election campaign was under way, with Roosevelt running for an unprecedented third term against Wendell Willkie, a liberal and anti-isolationist Republican. The campaign activated fanatical isolationism and spawned vicious anti-Semitism. The numerous pro-Nazi and anti-Semitic organizations that had mushroomed during the 1930s now accused the Jews of all sorts of evils and offenses, but especially of the desire to involve the United States in the European war. The anti-Semites even charged Roosevelt with being a concealed Jew. Anti-Semitism became so overt during the campaign that both Roosevelt and Willkie found it necessary several times to condemn anti-Semitism and the anti-Semites. Anti-Semitic candidates ran for Congress in several states (all were defeated).

The National Association of Broadcasters at this time

adopted a new code placing rigid limitations on broadcasts of "controversial public issues." Its effect was to make many radio stations cancel or fail to renew their contracts with Father Coughlin, who had been continuing to oppose America's lifting of the arms embargo and inveighing against aid to Britain. While some anti-Semitic and pro-Nazi groups began to disintegrate, anti-Semitism increasingly took the guise of isolationism.

The America First Committee was founded by conservative isolationists in 1940 shortly after the United States began to provide aid to England. It was soon infiltrated from both the left and the right. American Communists, loyal to the interests of the Soviet Union, then Germany's ally, were avid isolationists until Germany attacked the Soviet Union on June 22, 1941. The Socialists regarded the war as a capitalist-imperialist struggle and opposed America's participation in it. Norman Thomas, the party's perennial presidential candidate, was a member of America First's board. But the America First Committee proved more vulnerable to right-wing infiltration and it soon became a national platform for anti-Semitic propaganda whose main thrust was that the Jews were dragging America into war. Charles A. Lindbergh, the first pilot to have made a solo flight across the Atlantic, became the Committee's prized spokesman. In a speech at Des Moines in September 1941, Lindbergh charged: "The three most important groups which have been pressing this country toward war are the British, the Jewish, and the Roosevelt administration." Reciting the conventional anti-Semitic litany, Lindbergh described the Jews as the "greatest danger to this country" because of "their large ownership and influence in our motion pictures, our press, our radio, and our government." But public opinion was turning, and that speech injured both the cause and the reputation of the America First Committee. Many liberals, including Norman Thomas, resigned. When the Japanese bombed Pearl Harbor on December 7, 1941, the America First Committee crumbled. On December 8, Congress declared war on Japan. Three days later, Germany and Italy declared war on the United States.

EVER SINCE HITLER had come to power in Germany, American Jews watched with fear and foreboding as his shadow darkened Europe. Apprehensive about the fate of the Jews in Germany and Austria and in the other countries where anti-Semitism had become part of governance, they were also apprehensive about their own security at a time when it appeared that anti-Semitism was at flood tide in the United States. Nevertheless, American Jews tried repeatedly to influence Congress and the President to enact special legislation to bypass the immigration quota restrictions in order to admit Jewish refugees from the Third Reich. But they were too few and their allies insufficiently influential to effect any basic change in attitudes or policies. The Depression still lingered and the sullen xenophobic mood of the Depression lingered as both the American public and its legislative vehicle, the Congress, repeatedly rejected pleas to open America's doors a bit more wide even just for refugee children.

Insofar as their own resources were concerned, American Jews did not stint. They had long ago learned to give for Jews abroad. In 1939 the United Jewish Appeal was established for more efficient fund raising to meet the swelling needs of Jews overseas. The JDC sent moneys to the European Jews through every available channel, for by 1940 American Jews knew that the Polish Jews were being imprisoned in ghettos and subjected to a deliberate policy of starvation.

America's entry into the war raised Jewish morale, for most Jews had indeed hoped for America's intervention in the European war, believing that all Europe and especially the European Jews could be saved only by utterly crushing Hitler and the Third Reich. In 1939 and 1940 some young Jews had gone to Canada to enlist there in order to fight the Nazis as soon as possible. Once the United States was in the war, some 550,000 Jewish men and women, about 12 percent of the Jewish population, served in the armed forces. They suffered over 40,000 casualties, of which 8,000 were combat deaths. Some 36,000 received awards for bravery. For America's Jews, as for most Americans, taking part in that war, whether in the armed forces or on the home front, was a moral imperative. It was the quintessential just war.

The war and Germany's seizure of Europe shifted the center of Jewish institutional life from Europe to America. The seats of the Zionist movement were no longer in Berlin, Warsaw, and London, but now in New York and Jerusalem. The Yiddish Scientific Institute—YIVO—which had flourished in Vilna since 1925, moved its headquarters to New York in 1940, where, under its new name YIVO Institute for Jewish Research, it continued its scholarly work on East European Jewry. In 1941 the Agudath Israel, a European organization dedicated to the preservation of Judaism by strict observance of Halakah, moved its main office from London to New York. Yet at that critical juncture in Jewish history American Jewish institutions were unprepared and ill-equipped to assume the role of world Jewish leadership.

By the early 1940s American Jewry had become predominantly native, for a generation had passed since the restriction of immigration. The decades of secularism, radicalism, indifference to Judaism, had devitalized the Jewish community, drained its best talents. Able young Jews abandoned Jewish concerns in search of careers in the larger society and in the service of universal causes. The Jewish community was unable to produce leaders comparable to that extraordinary galaxy that had arisen at the beginning of the century. There were no successors to Jacob Schiff and Louis Marshall.

The old ideological divisions sharpened during the war. In the American Jewish Committee and in the Reform movement, descendants of the German Jews held rigidly to the view that they were Americans of Jewish faith, even though their commitment to that faith was often merely ceremonial. Concerned mostly for their own position and security, especially in that climate of raucous anti-Semitism, they nevertheless retained that traditional sense of stewardship for less fortunate Jews elsewhere. Still, they lacked the passion of Jewish fraternity that had animated men like Schiff.

The Zionists, whose movement had barely touched American Jews between the two World Wars, now came to life as a political force. The accelerating need of persecuted European Jews for places of refuge coupled with England's adamant policy of restricting Jewish immigration into Palestine appeared to validate the Zionist cause and dramatize its urgency. The leadership of the Zionist movement at that time was in the hands of American-born Jews, many of them in their sixties, for whom the terrible plight of the European Jews offered an opportunity for political triumph after years of impotence.

The Jewish leadership with closest familial and political ties to East European Jewry were concentrated in the Jewish Labor Committee and its associated groups (Workmen's Circle and the Jewish Labor Bund), in some Orthodox institutions, and in the Labor Zionist associations, all of whom still retained Yiddish in their publications and public meetings. For the most part, their leadership was composed of first-generation immigrants still not wholly at ease in America, still without sufficient access to people of influence in American politics.

The tragedy of the European Jews was the central issue

confronting the American Jewish organizations. It occupied their attention but that constant preoccupation proved inadequate to the extraordinary challenge of the time. Trapped by age in fixed views, unable to divest themselves of the habits and conventions of their past, American Jewish leadership tried but in the end failed to help the European Jews.

Under the pressure of events, the American Zionists called an extraordinary conference on May 9–11, 1942, in the Biltmore Hotel in New York City. Present were Chaim Weizmann, then president of the World Zionist Organization and of the Jewish Agency, and David Ben-Gurion, chairman of the Zionist Executive. With a new militancy, the conference adopted a series of resolutions, later called the Biltmore Program, whose chief objective was that Palestine should now be established as a Jewish state (a "Jewish Commonwealth"). The old ambiguous formula of "a Jewish national home in Palestine" was jettisoned for an aggressive policy. At this time the Jewish Agency opened an office in Washington, which was directed by Nahum Goldmann, a leading Zionist in pre-Hitler Germany and member of the Jewish Agency executive. The attainment of a Jewish state in the aftermath of the war now became the overarching goal of the Zionist movement.

JUST THEN, the great killing centers which the SS's Death's Head units operated began the systematic gassing of the European Jews. The first report of the gassings and also of the mass shootings of the Jews on Soviet territory since the summer of 1941 reached London in June 1942. Dispatched by the underground leaders of the Jewish Labor Bund in the Warsaw ghetto to the Polish government-in-exile, the report estimated that some seven hundred thousand Polish Jews had already been murdered and that the German government had indeed undertaken to carry out Hitler's threat to annihilate all the Jews in Europe. The Bund leaders asked the Polish government to use its influence on the Allied governments to have them undertake without delay a policy of retribution against Germans and fifth columnists living in their countries.

The Allies took no political or military action in response to that report, but the Polish government-in-exile and the British media disseminated it widely. The news reached the United States. On July 21, 1942, twenty thousand persons attended a rally at Madison Square Garden called by the American Jewish Congress, B'nai B'rith, and the Jewish Labor Committee, and chaired by Stephen S. Wise, longtime Zionist and president of the American Jewish Congress. Speakers included New York Governor Herbert H. Lehman, New York City Mayor Fiorello H. La-Guardia, AFL president William Green, and Bishop Francis J. McConnell, head of the Methodist Church in New York. In a message to the meeting, President Roosevelt declared that the American people would "hold the perpetrators of these crimes to strict accountability on the day of reckoning which will surely come." Protest meetings were later held in Boston, Chicago, Cleveland, Los Angeles, and St. Paul. On July 23, the ninth of Av, which the Synagogue Council of America proclaimed as a day of mourning, the House of Representatives opened with a special prayer for the Jewish victims of Nazi persecution. Protestant and Catholic clergy issued statements condemning the Nazi atrocities. Later the Orthodox rabbis of the United States and Canada proclaimed August 12 as a day of fasting and prayer for the persecuted Jews.

In the summer of 1942 information reached the State Department confirming that Hitler had indeed undertaken a systematic program to murder all the European Jews and that by then over two million Jews had been killed. The documents, which the State Department had withheld from the public, were finally released on November 25, 1942. A week later, on December 2, demonstrations were held across the United States. In New York City, half a million Jewish workers stopped work for ten minutes. Metropolitan radio stations observed two minutes of silence; the NBC radio network broadcast a memorial service.

On December 8, 1942, a delegation of Jewish leaders (American Jewish Committee, American Jewish Congress, B'nai B'rith, Jewish Labor Committee, and Union of Orthodox Rabbis) saw Roosevelt for not quite a half hour, presented him with a memorandum on the facts of the mass murder and proposed in their discussion a series of actions that might bring a halt to the killing.

In that same week, the State Department, most of whose functionaries were indifferent at best to the fate of the Jews, was studying a British draft text of a proposed Allied Declaration condemning the German annihilation of the Jews. On December 17, 1942, the United States, the United Kingdom, the Soviet Union, the French National Committee, and the governments-in-exile of Belgium, Czechoslovakia, France, Greece, Luxembourg, the Netherlands, and Poland, issued that declaration, the "German Policy of Extermination of the Jewish Race," which drew upon fully authenticated reports about the mass killings and concluded that the German authorities were "now carrying into effect Hitler's oft-repeated intention to exterminate the Jewish people in Europe." Condemning "this bestial policy of cold-blooded extermination," the signatories solemnly resolved "to ensure that those responsible for these crimes shall not escape retribution, and to press on with the practical measures to this end."

American Jewish leaders, realizing that the unprecedented calamity that had befallen the European Jews demanded their single-minded energy, took steps for joint action despite the fundamental ideological cleavages that

114

divided them. After months of ad hoc cooperation, the major Jewish organizations formally constituted a Joint Emergency Committee on European Jewish Affairs on March 15, 1943. In addition to their unremitting intercessions with American government officials, they drafted a comprehensive program for the rescue of the European Jews, which they planned to submit to the United States and the Allied governments.

Meanwhile, at Dr. Chaim Weizmann's initiative, preparations were under way to bring all Jewish organizations together in an American Jewish Conference that would consider the postwar Jewish agenda at the peace table: Jewish rights and security in post-Hitler Europe and the future of the Jews in Palestine. Though Hitler's plan to murder all the European Jews had become known and though reports of the killings continued to horrify the American Jews, at that time no one could yet conceive of a Europe without Jews. While American Jews were thus trying to submerge their differences in the interests of the European Jews, Jewish solidarity was then being disturbed from an outside source.

Shortly after the outbreak of the war, a handful of young Jews from Palestine engaged in a campaign on behalf of the Irgun Zvai Leumi, an extremist split-off from the Haganah, the Jewish settlement's underground military organization, came to the United States. (The outbreak of the war prevented their return home.) Associated ideologically with the Revisionist movement, a maximalist political Zionist group opposed to the World Zionist Organization, these young Palestinian Jews now began to campaign for the creation of a Jewish army, to consist of Palestinian and stateless European Jews, to help fight the Germans. They formed a Committee for a Jewish Army, whose leader and most dynamic personality was Hillel Kook, better known under his pseudonym Peter H. Bergson. With a flair for drama and publicity, Bergson managed to attract to his activities prominent Jews and non-Jews not previously associated with Jewish causes. His dashing resourcefulness made the mainstream Zionists look apathetic, while his political extremism and organizational irresponsibility put him on a collision course with the whole Jewish community. Nevertheless, his inventive, assertive tactics to gain public attention, like the frequent full-page ads in *The New York Times*, with their clamorous messages, evoked enormous responsiveness to the urgency of the Nazi threat among Jews who were beyond the reach of the traditional Jewish organizations.

That Jews were responsive to demands of the times was evident even in the Reform movement, which for nearly a half century had been untouched by the realities of American Jewish life. In 1942 the Union of American Hebrew Congregations, having been roused by a self-study, began undergoing an administrative and ideological transformation. The CCAR (Central Conference of American Rabbis), which had shifted from anti-Zionism to neutrality with regard to Palestine in 1935, had in 1942 adopted a resolution favoring the establishment of a Jewish army in Palestine to fight in the Middle East against the Axis powers. The composition of the Reform rabbinate was changing as younger men—many of them trained in the Jewish Institute of Religion under Stephen Wise—began to replace the old guard of German classical Reform Judaism.

But the Reform movement still nurtured some rabbis and laymen (a minority, to be sure) who were committed to a form of Jewish religious isolationism, divorced from a sense of common fate and fraternity with Jews outside America. Deploring "the growing emphasis upon the racial and nationalistic aspect of Jewish thought," a few dozen of these like-minded rabbis seceded from the CCAR to form, along with laymen who had seceded from the UAHC and the American Jewish Committee, a new organization called the American Council for Judaism. It began functioning in mid-1943 and operated essentially as a Jewish lobbying group against the creation of a Jewish state and, once the state was established, survived for a decade or two in the anomalous role as a group outside the general Jewish consensus.

Reports meanwhile kept pouring in from European sources that documented the unbelievable scope and unsurpassed horror of the mass murder of the Jews. Demonstrations, protests, days of prayer and mourning highlighted the lives of American Jews. On March 1, 1943, another demonstration, called by the American Jewish Congress, the AFL and the CIO, and other organizations, was held at Madison Square Garden, with 20,000 people inside and 75,000 crowding the streets outside. The assemblage adopted a resolution that called for the release of the Jews from German-occupied territories, the establishment of refugee sanctuaries, the revision of American immigration laws, admission of refugee Jews to Great Britain and British territories, the easing of Latin American immigration restrictions, admission of Jews to Palestine, provision of financial guarantees to countries serving as refuge, and, finally, punishment for the perpetrators of the mass murder.

Protests continued throughout the country. Resolutions were adopted in the Senate and House of Representatives. Jewish educators organized children's demonstrations. YIVO presented a petition, signed by 238 American scholars and scientists, to Roosevelt appealing for the rescue of the European Jews.

The British, in response to mounting pressure at home for rescue action, invited the Americans to confer with them. After weeks of negotiations, the Anglo-American Refugee Conference met in Bermuda, April 19–30, 1943. It was the very time the remaining Jews in the Warsaw ghetto rose up against their German oppressors. It was already too late to help them. No Jewish organizations, British or American, were invited to participate in the Bermuda conference or to send observers, but with unwarranted hopes the Joint Emergency Committee for Jewish Affairs submitted its rescue program and actively lobbied on its behalf among top U.S. officials participating in the Bermuda conference. They even pleaded with the British Foreign Secretary Anthony Eden.

The Bermuda conference accomplished even less than the Evian conference had, because neither Britain nor the United States was really prepared to undertake any major rescue action. The entire conference was seen to be a face-saving maneuver in response to public demands. Jewish reaction was bitter. Especially bitter were the Bergson group's full-page ads in *The New York Times*.

Having abandoned the campaign for a Jewish army, the Bergsonites now concentrated on rescue, even to the exclusion of a Zionist program. On July 26, 1943, they called a massive Emergency Conference to Save the Jewish People of Europe, which then transformed itself into an Emergency Committee to Save the Jewish People of Europe. Bergson and his friends embarked on a campaign that enlisted prominent Americans in government, the entertainment world, and the professions. Being outsiders, untrammeled by the responsibility or prudence that inhibited American Jewish leaders, and also profoundly touched by the tragedy of the destruction of the European Jews, the Bergson group moved without regard for consequences other than their objectives. In the next six months they electrified the American public by their public-relations and lobbying tactics. They rallied support among senators and congressmen to introduce a resolution dealing with the rescue of the European Jews and to hold hearings on the subject in both houses. Nothing came of these efforts because of more momentous developments within the Roosevelt administration itself.

Henry Morgenthau, Jr., Secretary of the Treasury, and members of his staff had for some time been concerned in the course of their official duties and as a matter of conscience with aid to the European Jews. They repeatedly ran into difficulties with the State Department in clearing or expediting various undertakings. After enduring months of delay in one case, the Treasury staff investigated and uncovered information showing that the State Department had knowingly pursued a policy of deliberate obstruction in aiding the European Jews. Meanwhile, in other discussions, Oscar Cox, Assistant Solicitor General, had suggested to Morgenthau that an interdepartmental agency ought to be created that could bypass the State Department and operate expeditiously to help the Jews. Milton Handler, an attorney on Cox's staff, drafted a proposal for such an agency. Armed with his staff's report on the State Department and the Handler draft, Morgenthau and two of his staff members went to see Roosevelt on January 16, 1944. Roosevelt agreed to their request. On January 22, 1944, the War Refugee Board was officially created. It was the first and only substantial program on behalf of the beleaguered European Jews to which the Roosevelt administration committed itself.

The American Jewish Conference, meanwhile, convened in New York City on August 29, 1943. Its original agenda was enlarged to include also immediate efforts on behalf of the European Jews. In that session as well as those in the following years, the different ideological and institutional interests of the several Jewish organizations collided. One by one, the Agudath Israel, the American Jewish Committee, and the Jewish Labor Committee withdrew from the Conference. While struggling to win over non-Zionist Jews to their objectives, the Zionists continued to wage war against the Bergson group, trying to discredit them by fair means and foul. The Bergsonites, for their part, once the War Refugee Board began to operate, reverted to their Revisionist politics. Before long their associates in Palestine were engaged in terrorist acts against the British.

In MARCH 1944, the Germans occupied Hungary. By now the world knew what could be the fate of Hungary's 650,000 Jews. Auschwitz was no longer an unfamiliar name. American Jewish organizations importuned the President and the State Department to save the Hungarian Jews. On March 24, 1944, Roosevelt issued a statement directed particularly to the Hungarians, warning that "none who participate in these acts of savagery shall go unpunished." British Foreign Secretary Anthony Eden issued a similar warning, but the Germans and their Hungarian accomplices were not deterred from their course. The efforts of the War Refugee Board to rescue some Hungarian Jews through possible routes via Yugoslavia to Turkey proved futile.

By the end of 1944 the terrible extent of the Jewish catastrophe had become apparent, but its implications for the Jewish future were as yet only dimly perceived. American Jews were practical people and so they turned their efforts toward postwar relief for the survivors, especially through the channels of the newly created United Nations Relief and Rehabilitation Administration (UNRRA). They began to lobby for special legislation to permit the immigration of surviving Jews from their European pestholes. (One minor wartime achievement was the creation in 1944 of the so-called "free port" at Oswego, New York, where about a thousand Jewish refugees from Italy found refuge outside the regular immigration channels.) The Zionists intensified their work on behalf of a Jewish state, though the center of Zionist action had now shifted to Palestine itself, where the Irgun's terrorist activities against the British exacerbated tensions not only between the British and the Jews, but within the Palestinian Jewish community and the Zionist movement.

As the Allied armies closed in on the Third Reich and the occupied countries were liberated, preparations went ahead to convene a United Nations Conference on International Organization at San Francisco on April 25, 1945. The American Jewish Committee and the American Jewish Conference were the two Jewish groups among forty-one other voluntary associations to be given consultant status. The Committee concentrated its efforts on a proposal for a human-rights commission; the Conference lobbied for a Jewish state in Palestine.

President Roosevelt did not live to see the war's end. He died on April 12 and was succeeded by Harry S. Truman. On April 30, Hitler committed suicide in his Berlin bunker. On May 8 the war in Europe came to an end. The Allies were victorious, but the Jews had lost the war.

# III

# RECOVERY
# AND RENEWAL

# 7

# *The Golden Age in America, 1945–1967*

THIS TIME, when the Americans came home from the war, they did not turn their backs on the world. The chief architect of the United Nations, the United States became its main financial support and provided the physical facilities for its operations. From V-E day until 1947, the United States spent over $11 billion in aid to UNRRA and from then until 1950, through the Marshall Plan for European Economic Recovery, disbursed $72.5 billion for foreign aid.

Committed to arraign the leaders of the German dictatorship for their bestial crimes before a world tribunal, the United States played the central role at the International Military Tribunal at Nuremberg, where the twenty-four surviving Nazi government and party leaders were tried and sentenced for war crimes and crimes against humanity. After that trial, the United States conducted a series of twelve other trials against special Nazi groups (*Einsatzgruppen*, industrialists, doctors and other medical personnel, ministries, etc.). A total of 836,000 Nazis were tried in the American Occupation Zone of Germany.

At home, American immigration policy, the long-held turf of America's xenophobes and anti-Semites, became a little more flexible by the enactment of emergency legislation, beginning with Truman's Directive of December 22, 1945, and later followed by the Displaced Persons Acts of 1948 and 1950, and by the Refugee Relief Act of 1953. Nevertheless, America's immigration law continued to adhere to the national-origins quota system, which was reaffirmed in the enactment, over Truman's veto, of the McCarran-Walter Act of 1952. Only with the passage of the Immigration Act of October 3, 1965, was that quota system, with its built-in racism, finally abolished. The new law established numerical ceilings on immigrant visas on a "first come, first served" basis and allowed a small preference for refugees.

Between 1944 and 1952 nearly 150,000 Jews immigrated into the United States, most of them East European Jews, survivors of the Third Reich's slave-labor and death camps. Thereafter, until 1965, almost 100,000 more Jews entered, coming primarily from Hungary, Egypt, Cuba and other Latin American countries, and also from Israel.

THE THIRD REICH had ended in the conflagration of the terrible war that it had set off. Its only lasting accomplishment was the murder of six million European Jews and the extinction of Ashkenazic Jewish culture on the European continent.

Yet the surviving Jews still remained in the whirlwind of history. In 1945 some 90,000 European Jews were living in displaced-persons' camps and in local communities in Germany, Austria, and Italy, waiting to find a home somewhere in the world. Polish Jews who had spent the war years in the Soviet Union were repatriated and, along with other Polish Jews who had been in hiding or with the partisans, returned in search of their homes, only to find themselves once more outcast and assaulted. The German occupation had taught the Poles that Jews could be murdered with impunity. From March 1945 to April 1946, more than 800 Jews who had hoped to start new lives once again in Poland were murdered by Polish pogromists. By the end of 1946 some 150,000 Jews fled Poland through Czechoslovakia into the DP camps of Germany and Austria, where they began once again to look for a new home.

Some got visas to the United States, others to Canada, to Latin American countries, to Western Europe and Australia. Tens of thousands left for Palestine, some with certificates issued by the British Mandatory. But many more went illegally, trying to bypass the British blockade. The British began to turn back the wretched, overcrowded ships, interning their long-suffering passengers in Cyprus. (Once, in the dramatic case of *Exodus 1947*, the British sent the refugees back to Germany.) Jewish immigration to Palestine and the establishment of a Jewish state now occupied the center stage of international politics. Accelerating tension and terrorism in Palestine prompted the British to relinquish their mandate, and early in 1947 they submitted the Palestine question to the United Nations for solution.

Meanwhile, American Jews, through their philanthropic institutions, took responsibility to provide for the needs of the displaced and refugee Jews in Europe—food, clothing, and shelter, medical care and education, transportation and resettlement—beyond the basic maintenance that UNRRA afforded. American Jews began to contribute for these purposes on an unprecedented scale. In 1945 all the federated fund campaigns throughout the United States raised nearly $57 million, double the amount raised in 1939, which they used entirely for goods and welfare. The next year, they raised over $131 million. At the same time, American Jews were giving not only philanthropy for humanitarian needs, but were contributing through other channels, privately and even surreptitiously, millions of dollars for arms purchases for the Palestinian Jewish settlement's struggle for independence.

American Jews, who had in the past been largely indifferent to Zionism, were now passionately committed to the goal of a Jewish state, a conclusion that the powerlessness of the European Jews during the war had tragically underscored and that the homelessness of the survivors reinforced. American Jewish leaders became convinced that a Jewish state in Palestine was a necessary political solution to a humanitarian problem, even though it might not necessarily resolve the anomalous condition of the Jews in the world.

In August 1947 the UN Special Committee on Palestine submitted its report to the General Assembly, calling for the partition of Palestine into an Arab and a Jewish state within an economic union. American Jews endorsed the plan wholeheartedly and Zionist and non-Zionist organizations alike lobbied energetically for American support. On November 29, 1947, with the United States and the Soviet Union both favoring partition, the UN General Assembly voted for it (33 for, 13 against, 10 abstaining), with Britain and the Arab states the principal opponents. No one disputes the fact that American Jewish energy helped to convince Truman and his advisers of the merits of partition. Above all, the ghosts of six million murdered European Jews haunted the chambers of the United Nations.

Britain had set May 15, 1948, as the day of her withdrawal from Palestine. While the Jews made plans for their state and the Arabs made plans for war, strife accelerated in Palestine. On the afternoon of May 14, 1948, when diplomatic efforts were still under way in the United Nations to find another solution to the Palestine problem that would appease the Arabs, the Jewish provisional parliament in Tel Aviv issued a declaration of independence: "By virtue of the natural and historic right of the Jewish People and the Resolution of the General Assembly of the United Nations, we hereby proclaim the establishment of the Jewish State in Palestine, to be called the State of Israel."

That midnight the British High Commissioner for Palestine departed and the British Mandate ended. A few minutes later President Truman gave de facto recognition to the new state. (Two days later the Soviet Union gave Israel de jure recognition.) The Arab states, refusing to accede, invaded the territory held by the Jews, but despite the Arabs' overwhelming numbers and weapons superiority, they could not vanquish the Israel Defense Forces. After issuing its declaration of independence, Israel successfully fought its war of independence. When armistice agreements were signed in 1949, Israel had more land than the United Nations had originally assigned. Its Arab neighbors continued their implacable refusal to recognize Israel's existence and its right to such existence.

For American Jews Israel had become the embodiment of the life force of the Jewish people. They lavished love and money on the young state whose fragile and precarious existence they wished to strengthen. In 1948, when Israel's very existence hung in the balance, American Jews, stirred by the urgency of history, raised over $200 million through their federated campaigns. All in all, from 1939 through 1967, American Jews raised over $3 billion for philanthropic Jewish needs, more than half of which went to Israel.

THE EXPERIENCES of the war years had had a transfiguring effect on American Jews and on their ideas of themselves as Jews. For countless numbers, induction into the armed forces launched their discovery or rediscovery of themselves as Jews. Away from the familiarity of Jewish home and Jewish neighborhood, flung into a non-Jewish milieu, the Jews in the armed services turned increasingly for the comfort of community to Jewish chaplains and local Jewish hospitality wherever they were stationed. They suddenly had a great hunger for all sorts of Jewish information. The National Jewish Welfare Board, which had been founded in 1917 to serve the religious needs of Jews in America's armed services, was called upon to provide enormous quantities of Bibles, prayer books, and the ABCs of Judaism and Jewish history. Over three hundred Jewish chaplains became teachers as well as rabbis to satisfy the craving for Jewish belongingness that had awakened in Jewish servicemen. For many, whether they fought in North Africa, Europe, or the Pacific, the daily confrontation with death stirred latent religious feelings, and despite the theologians' denigration of "foxhole religion," these feelings persisted in their later civilian life.

Thousands of American military men, Jews among them, helped to liberate the terrible camps at Buchenwald, Dora (Nordhausen), Dachau, and lesser places where the Third Reich had left a record of enslavement and death. That experience was seared into their memory and remained for decades as their witness to history.

Returning from the war, young people all over America got married and started to raise families. Jews did the same, though they tended to marry somewhat later than non-Jews and to have fewer children. Following a nationwide pattern, young Jewish families moved out to the suburbs of the large metropolitan areas where most of them had grown up. They also began moving westward, spreading more densely across the breadth of America. In 1957, 69.1 percent of American Jews lived in the Northeast, 11.9 percent in the North Central states, 11.3 percent in the West, and 7.7 percent in the South. By the late 1950s about 70 percent of all American Jews were native-born. That statistic presaged new directions for American Jewry.

Anti-Semitism in postwar America, according to public-opinion polls, declined to unprecedentedly low levels. Those anti-Semitic organizations that continued to operate conducted their activities on the fringes of society, without measurable impact on the country's social and political life. The chilling revelations of the German dictatorship's murder of the European Jews stripped away the facade of the polite prejudice and social superiority behind which anti-Semitism in the United States had often concealed itself. In post-Auschwitz United States, as indeed in most of the Western world, anti-Semitism no longer was morally acceptable.

In the 1950s colleges and universities that had a history of exclusionary and anti-Jewish policies now focused on academic achievement as a determining factor in their admissions. Soon Jewish students in substantial numbers were enrolled at all the Ivy League schools in the Northeast and their academic equivalents elsewhere in the United States. Continuing a long-established tradition, Jews pursued higher education as the means to economic success. As a group they had one of the highest levels of educational attainment. In the early 1970s about 75 percent of all college-age Jews were attending college.

The expansive tolerance in America's social life was matched by the expanding economy and the visibly rising living standards of the American people. America was becoming a middle-class country. Scientific discoveries and technological inventions created new industries and expanded economic horizons. Occupational and professional fields that had before been closed to Jews, and to other minorities as well, now opened to talent without discrimination. Though pockets of exclusion still remained in large industrial corporations, utilities, and banking in the two decades after World War II, Jews showed an extraordinary mobility as they concentrated increasingly in the professions, in managerial, executive, and proprietary positions in the economic structure. Their high occupational status yielded financial rewards and American Jews enjoyed a high per capita income, which was a consequence also of their high educational attainment and the quality of their professional training.

A remarkable rise in religiosity characterized postwar America, no doubt a consequence of the war experience. The percentage of Americans who belonged to churches and synagogues and who attended religious services rose substantially, a development no one in the secular 1930s would have predicted. American Jews shared in this return to religion. Living in suburban communities, often in newly created towns and in communities that had seldom seen Jews before, these native-born second- and third-generation Jews had to confront the question of their Jewish identity for themselves and even more for their young children. No longer able to live off the dwindling Old World capital of traditional Judaism that had sufficed for the immigrant Jews and their children, no longer satisfied as to the viability and transmittability of secular Jewish options that had attracted second-generation American Jews, the third generation turned to religion to give them a workable form of Jewish identity for themselves and their children. Unfamiliar with Judaism and largely ignorant of Jewish religious tradition, they turned in extraordinarily large numbers to the synagogue to provide them with the content and the forms of their Jewishness. The synagogue became, as it had been all through the Jewish millennial past, the prime vehicle of Jewish continuity.

New congregations were formed all over the United States. The congregants, in an era of rising affluence, began to build imposing synagogue structures whose architecture was often lavish and sometimes avant-garde, intended to reflect their members' status and aesthetic tastes. Synagogues proliferated. In 1955 some 520 congregations, estimated at 255,000 families, were affiliated with the (Reform) UAHC. The (Conservative) United Synagogue of America had 508 affiliated congregations with 200,000 families. The Union of Orthodox Jewish Congregations claimed a membership of over 700 congregations, and the National Council of Young Israel a membership of 72 congregations with 20,000 families.

The synagogue became the locus of all Jewish activity, the true Jewish center, the suburban reality of the 1950s, thus fulfilling Mordecai Kaplan's ideology of the 1930s. The synagogue was not only a place of worship; it was also a school for children, a recreational center for family and friends, a cultural center for the Jewish community at large, and the hub of local institutional activity.

The Conservative movement grew most rapidly in these years. It appealed particularly to third-generation Jews because it combined tradition and modernization, representing the happy medium between the immutability of Orthodox practices and the abandon of Reform antinomianism. The Conservative movement catered in just the right proportion to that inarticulated longing among third-generation Jews for the emotional reinforcement that traditional observance provided. Conservatism's powerful pull influenced also the course of the Reform movement, drawing it back toward the practice of a more traditional form of Judaism. No doubt under the influence of their members of East European ancestry, many new suburban Reform congregations began to restore some Hebrew to their service, to reinstate some of the liturgy that had been excised, and to encourage the return of certain traditional modes, like wearing head coverings in the synagogue.

While most Jews did not attend Sabbath services regularly, they did go with more frequency and in far larger numbers than had their parents. On High Holy Days the synagogues overflowed. *Bar mitzvah* and *bat mitzvah* (the equivalent ceremony for girls) became the most widely observed familial rite of passage, symbolizing the youngster's assumption of his Jewish identity and the successful outcome of his parents' attempt to rear him as a Jew.

While most American Jews no longer practiced Jewish law as prescribed by the Torah, large numbers observed circumcision, Jewish marriage, and burial, and vestigial forms of *kashrut* (abstaining from pork and other forbidden foods, for example). They were selective also in their observance of Jewish festivals, with Passover and Hanukkah—both child-centered and family-centered—as the most widely celebrated occasions, after the solemn High Holy Days.

The suburbanization of American Jews and the expansion of synagogues transformed Jewish education from being, as it had traditionally been, a communal enterprise (Talmud Torah) into a congregational one. In these years about 80 percent of Jewish children were estimated to have had some Jewish education, because their parents were affiliated with a congregation at least during those years their children attended the congregational school. The congregational school was sometimes just a Sunday school, supplementing the general education of the public school, but under the persistent efforts of rabbis and educators, it expanded its weekly hours of instruction to include two weekday afternoons in addition to the Sunday classes. While the Jewish school proved not entirely successful in teaching the substance of Judaism, Jewish history, Hebrew, or Bible, parents and teachers believed that it succeeded in inculcating in its pupils a sense of Jewish identity and a commitment to Jewish survival.

FOR TWO DECADES after the end of the Second World War, American Jews lived in peace and prosperity, their existence shaped by the progress in their socioeconomic status rather than by the intervention of history and crisis. But the changing balance of world politics jolted the Jews elsewhere in the world, and those tremors affected also American Jews.

The end of the Second World War marked the gradual decline of Britain, France, and Germany as major powers in international politics and heralded the emergence of the Soviet Union and the United States as the two great world powers. The Soviet takeover of Eastern Europe gave rise to grave tensions between the United States and the Soviet Union, commonly called the Cold War. In that struggle, the Soviet Jews, estimated to be about two million after losses of about one million during the war, became the victims of an escalating anti-Semitic campaign. The calculated Soviet attack on its Jews began right after the end of the war with charges of "cosmopolitanism," reflecting Stalin's paranoia about the sense of solidarity manifested by Soviet Jews toward Jews elsewhere in the world. The anticosmopolitan campaign was followed by the Communist campaign against "Jewish bourgeois nationalism," a charge that surfaced after Israel's establishment and the show of enthusiasm with which the Soviet Jews responded to the new Jewish state. In the ensuing years, at a time of widespread repression against all Soviet citizens, thousands of Jews were arrested, deported to slave-labor camps, or murdered for no reason but their Jewishness. All through the Soviet Union and its satellites, the state and party directed the most bizarre accusations of disloyalty against the Jews and terrorized their daily existence. Leading Communists, who had been born Jewish but whose lifelong priorities had been Communism rather than Judaism, were put on trial on fabricated charges of involvement in preposterous anti-Soviet plots. Soviet Jewish doctors were accused of having murdered Soviet leaders in the past and planning to do so in the future. A public trial was planned and preparations were under way to deport the Jews en masse to Siberia, a development providentially aborted by Stalin's death in March 1953. Those were the black years of Soviet Jewry.

Meanwhile the Communist takeover in China and the invasion of South Korea by Communist North Korea intensified America's tensions with the Soviet Union and reinforced America's long-held fears of Communism's worldwide aggressiveness. The revelations by Whittaker Chambers in 1948 of past Communist infiltration in high places in the U.S. government brought on the case against Alger Hiss. Then came the shocking disclosure of an espionage ring among American Communists who had passed atomic secrets to the Soviet Union. Distrust and animosity pervaded the country. America's cherished civil liberties seemed to be threatened by Senator Joseph McCarthy's intemperate and capricious anti-Communist investigations and by the anti-Communist legislation enacted by Congress. The prominence of Jews as Soviet spies in the trial of Ethel and Julius Rosenberg generated intense anxiety, as Jews feared that the hoary anti-Semitic stereotypes associating Jews and Bolshevism would be reawakened. Nevertheless, no appreciable rise in anti-Semitism was evident in the public-opinion polls, and Jews suffered no discernible prejudice or harassment.

Soviet aggressiveness in Eastern Europe and Asia, coupled with the staggering anti-Semitic campaigns let loose in the Soviet orbit, began to dissipate the illusions about the Soviet Union that many Americans, Jews among them, still held as a heritage of the wartime alliance and of the radical thirties. That process of disillusion culminated in 1956, when Nikita Khrushchev at a secret session of the Twentieth Congress of the Communist Party in Moscow denounced Stalin for those very crimes of which the West had long ago accused him. A few months later the Soviet Union suppressed an attempt at liberalization in Poland by the show of force and in Hungary Soviet troops crushed an attempted revolution. Thenceforth, Americans who were attracted to ideas and ideals of radical social change turned away from pro-Soviet movements, concentrating their energies in domestic civil-rights activities and in support of the emerging Third World nations.

PERSECUTED PEOPLES hope to avenge themselves on their persecutors; in this regard, as the story of Esther conveys to us, Jews are no different from others. Yet the recurring Jewish fantasy has been not of revenge against their persecutors but of the persecutors' repentance for the evildoing they committed against the Jews. It has been a dream of a world without anti-Semitism, of societies without murderous hate for Jews. The dream has not yet become a reality, yet on three historic occasions between 1951 and 1965 the drama of expiation for the crimes of anti-Semitism was enacted.

In 1951, when Germany was soon to sign a peace treaty with the four occupying powers (France, Great Britain, the Soviet Union, and the United States) and at the same time settle its prewar indebtedness, Konrad Adenauer, Chancellor of the Federal Republic of Germany, in an address to the West German parliament in Bonn, declared that the "unspeakable crimes perpetrated in the name of the German people" by Nazism imposed on the Germans "the obligation to make moral and material amends." His government was prepared to negotiate with representatives of the State of Israel and of world Jewish institutions "to bring about a solution of the material reparation problem in order to facilitate the way to a spiritual purging of unheard-of-suffering." The Bonn parliament, in a dramatic standing vote, unanimously endorsed the offer.

Jewish organizations from all over the world, with American ones dominant, formed a body called the Conference on Jewish Material Claims Against Germany, which became a third party to the negotiations that began in 1952 between the Federal Republic and Israel. The negotiations proceeded with relatively few obstacles, despite Arab opposition, and were concluded on September 10, 1952, with the signing of an agreement. The Federal Republic of Germany agreed to pay Israel the equivalent of $715 million in commodities and services, with an additional $107 million earmarked for the Claims Conference, to be paid out in the course of ten years. The moneys were to be used for relief and rehabilitation of Jewish survivors of the Nazi persecution; for cultural and education reconstruction, especially in the ravaged surviving Jewish communities in Europe; and for Holocaust commemoration and documentation projects. In 1964, when the Claims Conference made its final yearly allocation of funds, it established a Memorial Foundation for Jewish Culture, with $10 million for the support of "Jewish history, religion, education, traditions."

Some Jewish groups had opposed the negotiations and the acceptance of German moneys on the grounds that German guilt for crimes against the Jews was inexpiable. But Germany's readiness to pay this collective indemnity to the Jewish people, as represented by Israel and world Jewry, was widely accepted by the Jews as genuine expression of conscience.

Historic justice and redress were more fully realized when Israeli agents captured and kidnapped Adolf Eichmann from Argentina in 1960. Eichmann had been a middle-level bureaucrat in the Third Reich's Security Police whose responsibility was to schedule, organize, and manage the deportation of the European Jews to the killing centers. After the war's end, he told a colleague that the feeling of having killed five million Jews gave him so much satisfaction that he would jump laughing into his grave. But instead he was put on trial in Jerusalem for the murder of the European Jews. The trial opened on April 11, 1961, and closed on December 15, 1961, when the presiding judge read the court's sentence condemning Eichmann to death. After an unsuccessful appeal against the verdict and the sentence and after a futile appeal for clemency, Eichmann was hanged on May 31, 1962, his body cremated in accordance with the precedent set by the International Military Tribunal at Nuremberg.

The trial afforded Israel the opportunity to unfold before the world the full story of the murder of the European Jews by the Nazi regime in a way that had not been possible at Nuremberg, where that particular crime was subsumed in the category of crimes against humanity. In the United States the American public was riveted by the trial, and Eichmann became the personification of the murderer as bureaucrat. But the central message that emerged from the trial—that anti-Semitism was the driving force in the murder of the European Jews—was lost in universalizations about man's inhumanity to man.

The third occasion for expiation of the historic sin of anti-Semitism was amid the pomp and ceremony of the Second Vatican Council, commonly called Vatican II, convened in four sessions in Rome in the years 1962–1965. Originally called by Pope John XXIII and continued, after his death, by Pope Paul VI, the purpose of this ecumenical council was the spiritual renewal of the church (*aggiornamento*).

Preparations for Vatican II began just as Eichmann was being tried in Jerusalem. It was evident early on that the Church's attitude toward Jews and Judaism would be a subject on the agenda. The Secretariat for the Promotion of Christian Unity, headed by Augustin Cardinal Bea, was entrusted with the task of advancing dialogue and improving relations with non-Catholic Christians and also with Jews. In response to Cardinal Bea's interest, the American Jewish

Committee took the lead, followed later by other Jewish bodies, in submitting to his Secretariat memoranda dealing with the anti-Jewish elements in Catholic liturgy and the image of the Jews in Catholic teachings. The memoranda were prepared in consultation with Jewish scholars representing Orthodox, Conservative, and Reform viewpoints. (Orthodox Jewish institutions as such disapproved of Jewish efforts at dialogue and discussion with the Catholic Church.) Perhaps the single most influential Jewish figure in the discussions with Cardinal Bea was Professor Abraham Joshua Heschel of the Jewish Theological Seminary, a distinguished theologian with an enormous popular following among American Jews and Christians.

Bea's Secretariat began drafting a declaration on the Church's attitude toward the Jews. Its text became an arena of conflict, reflecting the tugs and pulls of noble and ignoble interests and motives in the Church. Strong opposition to a liberal position came from the powerful blocs of unreconstructed Christian anti-Semites within the Church and from Arab Christians as well as from Arab political groups outside the Church. After several revisions, the Church's statement on the Jews was submitted to the third session of Vatican II and approved on November 20, 1964, by a vote of 1,770 to 185. But as part of a larger declaration on the Church's attitude toward non-Christian religions, the document was still subject to textual revision.

From the Jewish perspective, it seemed that the declaration had undertaken to redirect the course of Catholic-Jewish relations. Its most powerful section declared:

Since the spiritual patrimony common to Christians and Jews is of such magnitude, this sacred synod wants to support and recommend their mutual knowledge and respect, a knowledge and respect that are the fruit, above all, of Biblical and theological studies as well as of fraternal dialogues. Moreover, this synod, in her rejection of injustice of whatever kind and wherever inflicted upon men, remains mindful of that common patrimony and so deplores, indeed condemns, hatred and persecution of Jews, whether they arose in former or in our own days.

May, then, all see to it that in their catechetical work or in their preaching of the word of God they do not teach anything that could give rise to hatred or contempt of the Jews in the hearts of Christians.

May they never present the Jewish people as one rejected, cursed or guilty of deicide.

All that happened to Christ in His passion cannot be attributed to the whole people then alive, much less to those of today. Besides, the church held and holds that Christ underwent His passion and death freely, because of the sins of all men and out of infinite love.

But the text of this extraordinary testament of atonement did not withstand the intensified pressure of extremist anti-Semites within the Church. Deprived by the sudden death of Pope John in 1963 of his luminous charity and love, the Church Fathers adopted a revised version that restricted, hedged, subtracted, and emasculated the earlier text. To the bitter disappointment of the Jews, it excised the sentence on deicide. Professor Heschel then declared that the Church's failure to condemn "the demonic canard of deicide" meant "condoning Auschwitz, defiance of the God of Abraham, and an act of paying of homage to Satan."

Despite its relapse from the earlier statement, the revised declaration received tempered public approval. It was, for all its shortcomings, clearly seen as a mandate to Catholics to heed and implement a new attitude toward Jews. In the United States, though disappointed with the text as revised, American Catholics nonetheless moved with high hopes toward fruitful dialogue with Jews as equal partners in matters of faith and brotherhood. Wherever the Church was responsive to change, the declaration encouraged them to improve relations with Jews. In countries where the Church was reluctant to move, the declaration was insufficiently implemented.

In 1954 AMERICAN JEWS marked the tercentenary of their presence in America. A policy statement issued by the commemorating committee highlighted the dual aspect of Jewish existence in the United States and the role of Jews in American society: their commitment to Judaism and Jewish survival and their dedication to social justice. "With our all-too-intimate knowledge of persecution," the statement declared, "we have brought a deep passion for human freedom and personal dignity. With our intimate knowledge of poverty and privation in the Old World, we have brought a striving for social justice and equality of economic opportunity."

As citizens concerned for the common welfare, in pursuit of their ideals of freedom and justice, Jews gave generously of their money and their energy to the National Association for the Advancement of Colored People (NAACP) and the National Urban League on behalf of equality for the blacks. They were the heart and sinews of the American Civil Liberties Union. They were more likely than others to be the liberals in the Republican Party, the reformers in the Democratic Party, the activists in the civil-rights movement, the absolutists in the civil-liberties movement, and the unflagging workers in radical groups.

In the mid-1950s a new kind of civil-rights movement came into being under the dynamic leadership of Martin Luther King, Baptist minister in Montgomery, Alabama. Passive resistance, boycotts, Freedom Riders, sit-in demonstrations attracted a new generation of civil-rights activists from the black community and also the white, with a high proportion of Jews among them. King's charismatic leadership succeeded in awakening widespread interest; early in 1963 a National Conference on Religion and Race met in Washington, at which Protestant, Catholic, and Jewish groups for the first time committed themselves to work together for racial justice. The March on Washington for Jobs and Freedom, held August 28, 1963, attracted nearly a quarter of a million Americans, white and black, Christian and Jew, and spurred the Congress to enact the strongest package of civil-rights legislation in American history.

Community action became the watchword of the civil-rights movement, and militancy gave it a new character. One program, the Mississippi Freedom Summer Project of 1964, ended tragically in the murder of three civil-rights workers, two of them Northern Jews, the third a Southern black. Later that summer, tensions in black slums in Northern cities erupted in a series of riots, in which hundreds of stores and businesses were looted and wrecked by rampaging blacks. In most places Jews were the chief targets of the violence. To be sure, Jews were not always attacked explicitly as Jews, but the evidence was strong that much of the rioting had a distinctly anti-Jewish flavor. Martin Luther King himself issued a statement deploring the presence of anti-Semitism in the riots, reminding his black constituency: "It would be impossible to record the contribution that the Jewish people have made toward the Negro's struggle for freedom—it has been so great."

The increasing militancy and violence of the black civil-rights activists and their antiwhite hostility began to tarnish the civil-rights movement and soon eroded its broad spectrum of support. The shift coincided with the escalation of America's role in the Vietnam War. Soon most white radicals, including Jewish universalists, turned their energy from civil rights to opposition to that war.

The tensions in the civil-rights movement between blacks and Jews were not reflected in the larger society, where Jews continued to move with confidence. They brought to American society their tradition of learning, their scientific curiosity, and their love of the arts. They were notable among the American Nobel prize winners and visible in America's scientific, cultural, and artistic communities. They were the innovators of television's entertainment industry. They constituted an influential segment of America's elite in the universities and in other opinion-molding circles. *Commentary*, a monthly journal founded by the American Jewish Committee in 1945, gained a reputation as a foremost intellectual periodical in the United States. Besides producing culture, American Jews, it was noted with some frequency, were also the most consistent supporters and avid consumers of highbrow and middle-brow culture. They bought books, visited art galleries and museums, went to the theater, and attended concerts in larger proportion than other groups.

The easy passage of American Jews into American society was a voyage into what an earlier generation had called "assimilation." It marked an erosion of ties to the Jewish community and found its ultimate expression in intermarriage. Available data, however limited or flawed, indicated a precipitous rise in intermarriage in the 1960s. Coupled with a sharply declining birthrate among Jews, intermarriage threatened Jewish continuity.

Yet intermarriage in the 1960s differed in one important regard from the classic cases of intermarriage in the past. Then it had served as a way out of the Jewish community. In the 1960s the data showed that in many intermarriages the non-Jewish partner converted to Judaism and the children of those unions were raised as Jews.

In the two decades since the end of the Second World War American Jews began to produce their own communal leaders, teachers, rabbis, and scholars. After the destruction of the East European Jews, for generations their demographic and cultural reservoir, American Jews now had to provide for themselves. Yeshiva University, the Jewish Theological Seminary of America, and Hebrew Union College expanded their programs. They opened branches in California and extended their programs to include, besides rabbinic training and ordination, training for cantors, educators, Jewish social and communal workers, and scholars. Brandeis University, founded in 1948 as a nonsectarian institution supported by the Jewish community, also developed a rich curriculum in Jewish academic and professional studies.

On the college and university campuses, Jewish studies proliferated. Once largely restricted to Semitics and Bible and offered at only a handful of schools, Jewish studies had become, since 1945, more and more accepted in most of America's prestigious colleges as part of the curriculum of a humanistic education. The range of course offerings was extended to embrace every aspect of Jewish studies—language and literature, history and social studies, Bible and rabbinics, religion and philosophy. The Jewish institutions of higher learning that were engaged in training Jewish scholars could scarcely keep up with the demand for them.

Israel meanwhile increasingly commanded American Jews' love and support. After the establishment of the state, the Zionist movement had declined in numbers and importance, but most American Jews would have identified themselves as Zionists in the sense that they were utterly pro-Israel. They took pride in Israel, in its achievements both in war with the Arabs and in wrestling with its desert environment. American Jews felt that their own image was enhanced by that of the Israelis as self-reliant and tough Jews, the image of the Jews as pioneers and warriors replacing the image of Diaspora Jews, often seen only as the object of contempt and persecution. The Israeli Jews, for their part, turned to American Jews for financial help and moral support. Still, despite mutual need, tension between the two communities simmered beneath the surface, largely because American Jews, though lavish with their love and money, chose not to settle in Israel. American Jews, for all their solidarity with the Israeli Jews, were convinced that America was different and that America was their home.

# 8

## *The Swinging Pendulum,*
## *1967–1981*

IN 1967 THE COURSE of Jewish history changed, entering an era of unpredictable crisis and an even more unpredictable Jewish revival. A generation had passed since the murder of the European Jews. The revulsion that the rotting corpses of the Third Reich's kingdom of death had produced all over the world was subsiding. There arose a new generation that knew not Joseph. A fresh cycle of anti-Semitism began with the Six-Day War of June 1967. It soon swept over Israel and the Jews in Eastern Europe, even the Jews in the United States.

THE YEARS OF TENSION between Israel and the Arab states and the Arabs' unremitting implacability led early in 1967 to a crescendo of Arab military threats against Israel's very existence. The Arabs tightened the noose around Israel, massing their troops on its borders and blockading Israel's access to the Red Sea. When the international community failed to relieve Israel's perilous entrapment, Israel moved with extraordinary swiftness to mobilize its army, and on

June 5 launched a preemptive offensive against Egypt, Jordan, and Syria. In six days of electrifying warfare on three fronts, Israel defeated its enemies and occupied the Gaza Strip and the Sinai peninsula of Egypt, the Golan Heights of Syria, and the West Bank of Jordan together with the Old City of Jerusalem, which Jordan had annexed back in 1949.

Israel's stunning military victory against the massive Arab forces, like David's subdual of the brute power of Goliath, seemed to signify the presence of God once again in Jewish history. Israel's repossession of the whole city of Jerusalem ignited a flame of religious passion among Jews in Jerusalem as all over the world, among secularists as well as believers, a passion one had thought modernity had all but extinguished.

Israel's success in liberating itself from the Arab stranglehold did not bring it acclaim from the world community of nations for its achievement or respect for its masterful self-defense, or even a sigh of relief that Israel and its Jews had been spared another destruction. As victors the Israelis no longer enjoyed the sympathy that they had once elicited as victims. The international crusade against Israel was led by the Soviet Union and its client states, the Arab nations, whom it had encouraged and armed for the attack on Israel. In the United Nations, Israel was condemned as an aggressor. Israel repeatedly offered to negotiate with its enemies, its price for the return of the Arab territories little more than acknowledgment of its right to exist and guarantees for a lasting peace, but the Arabs stubbornly rejected the outstretched hand of reconciliation.

Within its borders, the Soviet Union embarked on a new anti-Semitic campaign whose ugly propaganda did not distinguish between its Jewish citizens and the state of Israel, between Judaism and Zionism. Trofim Kichko, a Ukrainian and former Nazi collaborator elevated to the role of top anti-Semitic Soviet propagandist, charged in a widely disseminated book in 1968: "There is a direct connection between the morality of Judaism and the actions of the Israeli Zionists."

In Poland too, Israel's victory sparked the revival of anti-Semitism. From June 1967 until 1970 the Polish government and the Polish Communist Party gave free rein to a fury of anti-Semitism that began by driving the Jews from all government and party posts and ended by driving them from the country itself. By the time the anti-Semitic campaign had spent itself, barely five thousand Jews were left in Poland, where in 1939 there had been over three million.

Israel's isolation just before the Six-Day War and its pariah status afterward in the international community intensified the solidarity with it manifested by Jews everywhere in the world. Nowhere was that solidarity as unpredictably and sacrificially displayed as among the Jews in the Soviet Union. It had been thought that after fifty years of Soviet Communism, after the suppression of Jewish tradition and learning, after decades of isolation from the Jews in the world, the sense of Jewishness would vanish among Soviet Jews. It had been expected that the Soviet Jews, caught in the vise between a calculated policy of forced assimilation and a policy of willful and expedient anti-Semitism, would cease to be Jews. But the cunning of history defies prophecy. Jewish consciousness flared up out of the memory of the Holocaust, symbolized in the murderous events of Babi Yar in 1941, when the Germans with their Ukrainian collaborators in two days murdered over thirty-three thousand Jews of Kiev. Jewish consciousness was recharged by love and longing for that fragile Jewish state that the Soviets hated beyond reason.

The defiance of the Jews grew slowly, first with a handful of courageous people who decided that they would rather be Jews than Russians. They denounced Soviet anti-Semitism and demanded the right to emigrate to Israel, where they could lead full Jewish lives. In 1970 a group of Jews in Leningrad attempted to hijack a Soviet plane to take them to Israel. (They were caught, tried, and severely sentenced.) Never before had the Jews—or any other group—offered such resistance to the Soviet regime. Their movement, which concentrated only on the demand for emigration—"Let my people go"—grew, spreading all over the Soviet Union. The regime harassed the Jewish dissidents, arrested them, sent them away to camps, yet unpredictably and inexplicably the Soviets began to issue exit permits, presumably to those whom it wished to be rid of. In 1968 and 1969 small numbers left; in 1970 one thousand Jews emigrated. Then, as if the dam had burst, thousands upon thousands of Jews applied to leave. In the course of ten years' time about 150,000 Soviet Jews succeeded in getting the necessary papers to emigrate and to overcome the arbitrary and unmerciful obstacles that the Soviet KGB put in their way. In the early years most emigrants went to Israel. More recently, many have chosen to live in the United States.

As for the American Jews, living in a free country, their assertion of solidarity with Israel required little heroism, but it was not without its drama. American Jews closed ranks. As Israel's fate hung in the balance during the weeks when the tension was building before the Six-Day War and thereafter, they cast their lot wholeheartedly with Israel and its people. They gave their love, their support, their prayers, their money. Many volunteered for civilian service in Israel. There was a renewed sense of Jewish interdependence and a resolve that this time, unlike the time during the Second World War, American Jews would not fail to succor fellow Jews. The repressed guilt for the failure to have rescued the European Jews that had burdened Jewish consciences rose to the surface and found its release in an aggressive Jewish commitment. "Never again," the crude, immature slogan of the Jewish Defense League, an organization of young militant Jews formed in 1968, bespoke the new mood of Jewish assertiveness. American Jews were responding to Israel's exigent needs and to their sense that being Jewish was as important to them, perhaps even more important, than being American. For America's culture and politics were then in upheaval and the changes in American society were creating a milieu in which Jews no longer felt at ease, no longer felt quite at home.

THE UNITED STATES was being taken over by its youth, the dominant age cohort of the late 1960s. That youth culture in its several variants infected the adult world and polluted the country's political life. For nearly a decade American society was in turmoil, divided, bitter, and violent.

The counterculture, the product of white middle-class youth, was a new religion that pervaded American life. Its apostles were the Beatles, who offered the attainment of heaven on earth through the sacraments of rock music and drugs and the rites of sex. The faithful let their hair grow, wore blue jeans, and practiced vegetarianism. They were the flower children and the hippies, the dropouts from school and work, the runaways from home and family, in search of freedom—a mythic freedom from human relationships, from responsibility, from adulthood. They left home to join communes; they left their parents for gurus; they left the despised familiarity of their own religious culture in search of exotic Eastern cults. They experimented with sex, love, marriage, and family.

Passive, nonpolitical, nonintellectual, these children of the counterculture were manipulated by the New Left, which had emerged from the white community-action groups of the civil-rights movement. Born out of an American variant of passive resistance, the New Left sectarians were seduced by a mystique of force and violence cultivated by Third World and Latin American revolutionaries. The New Left rejected the Communism of the Soviet Union, but were attracted to Chinese and Cuban Communism, which they romanticized and idealized in much the same way that fellow-travelers in the 1930s had responded to Russia. As the United States grew more involved in the Vietnam War, the New Left turned from community action and propaganda to force, to politics by confrontation. Peaceful demonstrations gave way to violent demonstrations, to calculated destruction, or attempted destruction, of government facilities and scientific installations. Civil disobedience and draft resistance accelerated.

The civil-rights movement too had changed its colors. Having ousted its white sympathizers and supporters, it turned black-nationalist and radical, its militancy degenerating into violence. The Black Panthers, whose early programs provided free breakfasts for poor black children, soon became the black civil-rights equivalent of the Weathermen, the New Left's underground terrorist arm. In 1967 a new wave of black urban riots swept Northern cities. "Burn, baby, burn" became the militants' slogan. Black leaders fell into a pattern of justifying the arson and looting as legitimate black responses to social injustice. The cumulative and ultimate effect was the public's abandonment of the cause of civil rights and their withdrawal of financial support even from the moderate black civil-rights agencies.

The New Left, however, succeeded in its perverse goal of unsettling America's political life and institutions. The increasing turmoil over the Vietnam War that the New Left generated drove Lyndon Johnson from the White House. He decided not to seek reelection in 1968. That summer the

Democratic Convention, in the midst of turmoil and violence created by the New Left Yippies (Youth International Party) and the hippies, nominated Hubert H. Humphrey as their presidential candidate. Though Richard M. Nixon was the Republican candidate and long regarded as an enemy of the Left, enormous numbers of the youth cohort chose to sit out that presidential election, because they regarded Humphrey as President Johnson's tool. Humphrey lost by a bare half-million votes, 0.7 percent. Nixon won, having pledged to end America's participation in the Vietnam War honorably and to restore law and order at home.

In the course of the next four years, the New Left moved from confrontation politics to infiltration, to work, as they put it, "within the system." In 1972 they succeeded in getting Senator George McGovern nominated as the Democratic candidate for president. McGovern, regarded as a left-liberal, was an early opponent of the Vietnam War and pledged to dismantle America's military defense arrangements. Though the Democratic Party was the majority party, President Nixon, running for a second term, defeated McGovern in a near landslide. The New Politics almost destroyed the Democratic Party. Its radicalism shattered the Democratic coalition of the urban working class, Catholics, blacks, Jews, and the South that had existed for nearly half a century.

Jews had been one of the most loyal constituencies in that coalition. Though no longer among the urban proletariat, Jews had been voting Democratic in the same high proportion as the poor, the blacks, and the Hispanics. The McGovern candidacy altered that pattern. Some 81 percent of Jews had voted for Humphrey in 1968, but only 65 percent voted for McGovern. Barely 17 percent of Jews had voted for Nixon in 1968, but 35 percent did in 1972. Jews had come to perceive that the New Politics did not respond to their needs and interests, that indeed it was committed to policies and programs that were inimical to Jewish interests at home and abroad.

IN THE NEW LEFT, the Six-Day War released a torrent of hitherto subdued anti-Jewish sentiment. Maoist leftists in the United States copied lurid anti-Semitic propaganda from Arab sources. Black-nationalist radicals, in their own organizations and at New Left and New Politics meetings, agitated against the "imperialistic Zionist war." The New Left's alignment with the Third World nations and its growing hostility to Israel shocked the Jews within the movement. That disillusionment of 1967 was a historic re-enactment of the bitter disappointment that the Russian Jewish radicals had suffered in 1881 when their colleagues in the revolutionary movement applauded the peasants for pogromizing the Jews.

In Jewish experience, in the United States as elsewhere in the world, anti-Semitism had traditionally been the power tool of the Right, of political reaction and of fascism. But the Soviet Union incontestably demonstrated that the Left could practice anti-Semitism with as sharp a cutting edge as the Right. Soviet anti-Semitism soon coalesced with the Arab hatred of Israel and spread to the Third World nations. It found its most uninhibited expression at the United Nations. In the United States, that leftist anti-Semitism, as adopted by black nationalists and the New Left, was something new. American Jews, familiar with the anti-Semitism of the Ku Klux Klan and the minuscule hate groups like the American Nazi party and the National States Rights party, were now stunned by the explosion of anti-Semitism that erupted in the black community.

Its explicitness was a product of the changed climate in the United States that the student demonstrations of the 1960s had helped bring about. In the 1960s "free speech" had come to mean freedom from the restraints of civility and common decency. Every expression of abuse, scurrility, obscenity, and incitement to violence was permitted. In that milieu, black anti-Semitism came across loud and clear. In 1968, in a strike conducted by the United Federation of Teachers against the Board of Education because a local governing board (largely black) had fired many of its teachers (mostly white and Jewish), anti-Semitism soon overshadowed the fundamental issue of the strike—job security. Though the strike was eventually settled, it left permanent scars. Relations between blacks and Jews at work and in the neighborhoods they shared kept deteriorating. Ten years later it was a commonplace to hear blacks publicly attack New York City's Mayor Edward Koch as a "dirty Jew bastard" because, at a time of the city's financial crisis, he had cut back on certain programs that blacks regarded as their entitlement.

World events did not brake the accelerating disquiet that Jews felt. On Yom Kippur, October 6, 1973, when Egypt and Syria attacked Israel, she stood once again almost alone in the world. It took a full week before the United States agreed to resupply Israel's arms to make up for the terrible losses suffered because of the antitank and antiaircraft missiles the Soviet Union had supplied to the Arabs. Most European nations—including NATO members—refused to help Israel or even speak up in her behalf. Israel managed on its own to halt the Arab advance. The American airlifted supplies enabled her to launch a counteroffensive that ended in an encirclement of the Egyptian army.

Since 1967 the UN had become the seat of anti-Israel agitation. In the wake of the Yom Kippur War, which did not, as the Arabs and their Soviet sponsor had hoped, end in Israel's annihilation, the hatred against the Jewish state redoubled. In 1974 the Palestine Liberation Organization

(PLO), a terrorist Arab body committed openly to Israel's destruction, was invited to participate in the UN General Assembly's deliberations on the Palestine question and its head Yasir Arafat was invited to address the Assembly. Thereafter, the PLO had participatory observer status at the UN.

In 1975, Cuba, South Yemen, Libya, Somalia, and Syria—all Soviet clients—introduced in a debate in the UN an amendment to a routine resolution, declaring that "zionism" (lower case) was "a form of racism and racial discrimination." Some years back the Soviet Union had first proposed to link Zionism with racism and such resolutions had several times been offered, but had been defeated. In 1975, however, the hatred of Israel and the Jews had generated enough votes to pass such a statement. The resolution was adopted by a vote of 72 to 35, with 32 abstentions. It soon became incorporated in the UN's standard rhetoric.

Meanwhile, a new question arose to disturb the social peace within the United States: the introduction of quotas—sometimes called preferential treatment or affirmative action—in hiring and promoting members of certain racial minorities and of women. The intent was to rectify the proportional racial imbalance that past discrimination against these groups had created. The government, under the authority of the Civil Rights Act of 1964, established guidelines for hiring and promoting minority members that extended to colleges, universities, and professional schools as well as to government agencies. Private industry too came under such regulations. Quotas were introduced in determining student admissions to colleges, universities, and professional schools.

It soon became apparent that compliance with the regulations, in favoring some groups, injured the chances of individuals not in those groups in their pursuit of jobs, promotions, and school admissions. People better qualified or more experienced than members of minorities were sometimes passed over. Public debate and legal test cases soon heightened the tension between blacks, the chief beneficiaries of the quota system, and whites, especially at a time when the American economy was in a recession and opportunities were fewer than in the past.

The use of quotas raised fundamental questions that Americans had thought were long ago settled—that in America race per se was not a criterion by which to judge people; that the ideal of a color-blind society was still valid; that ability and performance, rather than race, should determine suitability for work or school. For Jews the legitimation of quotas, even if labeled "benign," traumatically evoked their own history as the victims of exclusionary quotas. Since they were less than 3 percent of the population, they would, under a quota system, have little chance of advancement. It is too soon to know if Jews have been hurt by these quotas, but one thing was certain: malaise spread among American Jews. It was an unlocalized discomfort, a sense of their growing unease in America.

In 1979 black anti-Semitism reached its climax. Andrew Young, a former civil-rights leader and black congressman from Atlanta, as U.S. Ambassador to the United Nations, held an unauthorized meeting with a PLO official in New York. His action, inconsistent with official American policy, was kept secret from the State Department. When news of that meeting became public, Israel responded angrily and American Jewish organizations, dismayed by an apparent betrayal of American policy, protested to President Carter. Secretary of State Vance reportedly told the President that Young had damaged United States–Israel relations and that he would have to go. Young resigned.

His resignation unleashed a rage of anti-Semitism in the black community. Blacks everywhere blamed the Jews, believing that they had forced Carter to ask for Young's

157

resignation. President Carter failed to defuse black anger, as he might have, by publicly explaining that Young's resignation was required as a matter of highest government policy, that it was not an exaction of the Jews. His neglect to do so and his praise of Young as a public servant added to the disquiet that American Jews felt over the incident. But it was not the raucousness of black anti-Semitism that disquieted the Jews so much as the import of Young's secretive meeting with a PLO representative.

Just a few months earlier Carter had helped bring to a conclusion the momentous course of events that Egypt's President Anwar Sadat had initiated in 1977. Egypt and Israel signed a peace agreement at Camp David. But Carter was now dissipating the political capital that he had accumulated in expediting the negotiations between Israel's Prime Minister Menahem Begin and Sadat. The Young affair bore out suspicions that Carter was shifting U.S. policy in favor of the PLO, despite the PLO's history of terrorism, despite its refusal to accept Israel's existence.

It was to be expected that such a departure would move the Jews to reconsider their loyalty to Carter and indeed to the Democratic Party, which by 1980 no longer seemed to be the same party that had once commanded such Jewish allegiance. In the presidential election of 1980, Carter took only 45 percent of Jewish votes, the first Democratic presidential candidate since John W. Davis in 1924 to fail to win a majority among Jewish voters. Ronald Reagan, the Republican candidate, who was strongly committed to Israel as a strategic ally of the United States in the Middle East, received 39 percent of Jewish votes, the largest any Republican presidential candidate ever won from Jews since Abraham Lincoln was elected in 1860.

THE CHANGING political behavior of American Jews reflected the new Jewish assertiveness that arose after the Six-Day

War and the openly acknowledged pursuit of Jewish self-interest. In other aspects of their life, however, which affected demography, education, and occupation, the Jews continued to act as they had in earlier decades. The Jewish birthrate declined below the replacement level. Intermarriage kept increasing, but so did the rate of conversion to Judaism by the non-Jewish partners in those mixed marriages. Jews continued to pursue higher education (nearly every Jew of college age was going to college), and Jews attained financially rewarding and prestigious positions. Jewish talents continued to enrich American culture. Saul Bellow won the Nobel prize for literature in 1976, and Isaac Bashevis Singer won it in 1978.

In their religious behavior, as in their political behavior, Jews acted out their outspoken affirmation of their Jewishness and their more intensely felt Jewish commitments. Traditional Judaism—Orthodoxy—which for decades had been pronounced dying, if not dead, the possession only of the old and the alien, came alive, unpredictably, implausibly. In the decade after the Six-Day War Orthodoxy emerged youthful and vigorous to transform the landscape of American Judaism. (A similar phenomenon was evident also in Israel and, less visibly but nonetheless unmistakably, also in the countries of the English-speaking Diaspora.)

Revived Orthodoxy was the product of cross-fertilization, paradoxicality, and heterodoxy. Its origins were indelibly foreign and indigenously American. Its energy derived from the most inflexible tradition and from alienation. It was an outgrowth of the counterculture and, at the same time, a recoil from it. The soil out of which the new Orthodoxy grew had been brought from Eastern Europe after the Second World War by survivors of the Holocaust, mostly, though not exclusively, Hasidim. Having outlived the gas chambers of the Third Reich and the Gulag of the Soviet

Union, they brought to the United States their traditions, their learning, and above all their passion for Judaism. They built *yeshivot* and day schools with sacrificial effort. They shamed the established American Orthodox and Conservative institutions by their passion and, by example, vitalized them.

The *baal teshuvah*, the returner to Judaism or to a more intense observance of it, became a commonplace phenomenon. No single factor explains how, suddenly it seemed, the return to Judaism had become not just an individual phenomenon but a social one. Just as there were many motives for the return, so there were many degrees and variations in the character of that return. The returners were of all ages and all kinds of backgrounds, but the most spectacular were those who returned from the brink, as it were.

When the counterculture began to seduce young Jews, the Habad movement of the Lubavitch Hasidim undertook to save their souls. Other sectarian Orthodox groups followed suit. They addressed the dropouts and the runaways not as minatory parents, but tempted them with authenticity, with a return to wholeness by way of their own tradition and a community of love among their own people. Statistics are lacking, but the right-wing Orthodox and the sectarians rescued and recruited thousands. Their active presence and their confidence in their faith disturbed the self-content of the secularists.

The counterculture, meanwhile, had penetrated into traditional Jewish bastions and the effect was to radicalize Judaism. In the Conservative movement, young people who were alienated by the bigness and lifelessness of the synagogues in which they had been reared began experimenting with *havurot*, small fellowships whose practice of Judaism would provide religious intensity and communality. The Orthodox equivalent was the revival of the *shtibl*, the East European Hasidic prayer house, which offered intimacy and immediacy without the synagogue's institutional accouterments. Orthodox young people sought also to make their movement responsive to contemporary society, even quixotically attempting to change Jewish law. On college campuses, on big-city streets, in hospitals and scientific laboratories, young Jews wearing *kippot* demonstrated their Jewishness. Kosher eating houses were established at many colleges and even Princeton University, whose eating clubs had once been the stronghold of anti-Jewish exclusivity, harbored a kosher eating club.

In one of history's lesser ironies, the feminist movement, which began by assaulting traditional Judaism because it treated women differently from men, soon inspired women to enhance their literacy in Judaism, if they were to attain equality. Committed Jewish women began to pursue higher Jewish learning, even to aspire to the rabbinate. The Reform movement trained women as rabbis and cantors and a few Reform congregations even engaged them. The Conservative movement extended women's rights in the synagogue, but balked at admitting them to rabbinical training.

The vigor of the new Orthodoxy spread throughout Judaism. It marked a new departure for American Jews in their relation to American society. The new Orthodox were not self-conscious about publicly demonstrating their Jewishness. They were ready to pay the costs that the separatism of their religious observance required. To be sure, like generations of American Jews before them, the new Orthodox made their accommodations to America, but they drew firmer lines than had their predecessors. They chose to be Jews on their terms and they were asking America to accept them on those terms.

# EPILOGUE

## In the
## Light of History

THE HISTORY OF the Jews in the United States has been—so far—a history of good times, of expectations realized. There were times of trial and trouble, but even at their worst, they never compared in scope or in malignancy to the calamities that befell the European Jews. In the United States Jews prospered as never before in their history.

The United States was the first country in the world to give the Jews political equality and religious liberty, enabling them, as no other nation-state had, fully to exercise their rights as citizens and, at the same time, freely to observe their religion, sustain their traditions, and perpetuate their culture.

Despite Jewish fears that America's freedom would subvert Judaism and seduce Jews from their faith and their people, the historic experience has been that most American Jews have chosen of their own volition to be Jews and to raise their children as Jews. America has demonstrated that Judaism can flourish in a free society, and the freedom of America has further demonstrated the vitality and adaptability of Judaism. In the words of the foremost scholar of Judaism, Gershom Scholem, "Judaism has proved itself infinitely adaptable without losing its original impetus." American Judaism, for all its divergencies from the Judaism of Eastern Europe before the Holocaust or from the Judaism of Ashkenaz during the Crusades, is still recognizably the same Judaism, sharing with them the common ancestry of biblical Judaism.

America has demonstrated also that Judaism can flourish in an open and pluralist society. A confident and affirmative American Judaism has engaged the larger society—secular and Christian—and emerged from that engagement intact and enriched. The interplay of living cultures stimulates growth that stultifying immurement inhibits. The American Jewish experience, still in process, still vulnerable, still experimental, has so far shown that with the will to do so, Jews can preserve and sustain Judaism and Jewish culture while participating in the larger society. Each Jew finds for himself the precise calibrations by which he can maintain the fine balance he wishes to achieve between living in the general society and living as a Jew. That is what life in a genuinely pluralist democracy entails.

Winthrop S. Hudson, professor of history at the University of Rochester and widely regarded as the dean of American church historians, has celebrated this rare achievement of American Jews. In the concluding chapter of his book *Religion in America*, he wrote:

> Perhaps one of the greatest contributions of Judaism to the United States will be to help other Americans understand how the United States can be a truly pluralistic society in which the pluralism is maintained in a way that is enriching rather than impoverishing, a society in which the integrity of different faiths is preserved while adherents of the several traditions engage

in open dialogue that will clarify and deepen their own self-understanding. A pluralistic society is a society of dual commitments which need not be in conflict but can be complementary. But whether conflicting or complementary, the citizen of a pluralistic society must bear the burden of both commitments. From the long experience of Judaism, Americans of other faiths can learn how this may be done with both grace and integrity.

# Appendices

# APPENDIX A

*Growth of the*
*Jewish Population in the*
*United States**

| Year | Estimated Jewish population | Percent of U.S. population |
|---|---|---|
| 1790 | 2,500 | 0.03 |
| 1818 | 3,000 | 0.03 |
| 1826 | 6,000 | 0.06 |
| 1840 | 15,000 | 0.1 |
| 1848 | 50,000 | 0.2 |
| 1860 | 150,000 | 0.48 |
| 1877 | 250,000 | 0.52 |
| 1888 | 400,000 | 0.6 |
| 1897 | 938,000 | 1.3 |
| 1900 | 1,058,000 | 1.4 |
| 1907 | 1,777,000 | 2.0 |
| 1917 | 3,300,000 | 3.3 |
| 1927 | 4,228,000 | 3.6 |
| 1945 | 4,771,000 | 3.7 |
| 1957 | 5,179,000 | 2.8 |
| 1970 | 5,870,000 | 2.9 |
| 1980 | 5,920,900 | 2.7 |

* Since the U.S. Census Bureau does not canvass the religion of the American population, the figures for the Jewish population are estimates. These statistics have been compiled from the *American Jewish Year Book*.

# APPENDIX B

## Important Events in American Jewish History

1788      The U.S. Constitution is ratified by the requisite nine states.

1789      On April 21 George Washington is inaugurated first President of the United States.

1790      The Newport congregation sends a letter of welcome to President Washington.

1791      The Bill of Rights becomes part of the Constitution.

1802      Rodeph Shalom, the first synagogue in America to follow the Ashkenazic rite, is established in Philadelphia.

1824      The Reformed Society of Israelites, the first American attempt of Reform Judaism, is organized in Charleston, South Carolina.

1826–1828   The disabilities of the Jews are removed from the Maryland Constitution.

1836   The migration of Jews to America from German lands begins.

1840   Jews assemble in New York and Philadelphia to protest the blood libel against Damascus Jews. Abraham Rice, the first rabbi to come to America, heads a congregation in Baltimore.

1843   The B'nai B'rith is founded in New York City. Isaac Leeser begins to publish *The Occident.*

1846   Isaac Mayer Wise arrives in America and heads a congregation in Albany, New York.

1847   Congregation Beth El, the first synagogue founded by East European Jews, is established in Buffalo.

1850   A Young Men's Hebrew Literary Association is founded in Philadelphia.

1852   The first East European congregation in New York is organized (later known as the Bet Hamidrash Hagadol, "The Great Synagogue").

1854   Isaac Mayer Wise becomes rabbi of Congregation B'nai Yeshurun in Cincinnati, where he remains until his death; he begins to publish *The Israelite.*

1859   In November the Board of Delegates of American Israelites is organized, the first attempt by American Jews to unite in defense of Jewish rights overseas.

1860     On February 1, the Thirty-sixth Congress is
         opened by the invocation given by Rabbi
         Morris J. Raphall of Congregation B'nai
         Jeshurun of New York.
         On November 6, Abraham Lincoln is elected six-
         teenth President of the United States.

1861     On April 12, the Civil War begins when Confeder-
         ate forces fire on Fort Sumter in Charleston
         Harbor.

1862     As a consequence of Jewish lobbying and the inter-
         vention of the President, Congress amends the
         law that specified that army chaplains were to
         be ministers of "some Christian denomina-
         tion"; it now reads, "some religious de-
         nomination."
         On December 17, General Ulysses S. Grant issues
         Order No. 11, expelling Jews from the area
         under the jurisdiction of the Union Army's
         Department of Tennessee.

1863     On January 7, under orders from President Lin-
         coln, Grant rescinds Order No. 11.

1865     The Civil War ends on May 26.
         The Thirteenth Amendment, abolishing slavery, is
         ratified by twenty-seven states and goes into
         effect.

1866     The Ku Klux Klan is founded to restore "white
         supremacy."

1873     Isaac Mayer Wise organizes the Union of Amer-
         ican Hebrew Congregations.
         The Panic of 1873, following the demonetization of
         silver, launches a new cycle of anti-Semitic
         propaganda.

1874      The first Young Men's Hebrew Association is formed in Philadelphia.

The United Hebrew Charities is organized in New York City.

Katriel Sarasohn begins to publish *Di Yidishe Gazetn* in New York City, the first Yiddish weekly to take hold.

1875      Isaac Mayer Wise founds Hebrew Union College in Cincinnati.

1877      Joseph Seligman is refused admission to the Grand Union Hotel in Saratoga, New York.

1879      Congress passes the Chinese Exclusion Act.

1881      Czar Alexander II is assassinated in St. Petersburg. In April a wave of pogroms spreads across Russia, launching mass emigration of Jews.

1882      The so-called May Laws are enacted in Russia; their discriminatory anti-Jewish policies intensify Jewish flight from Russia.

In August the first professional performance of a Yiddish play is given in New York; the cast includes a young actor, Boris Tomashefsky.

1883      Emma Lazarus writes a sonnet, "The New Colossus," which is later inscribed on the Statue of Liberty.

1885      Reform rabbis meeting in Pittsburgh adopt a radical statement of principles of Judaism, called the Pittsburgh Platform.

Katriel Sarasohn launches the *Tageblatt* in New York, the first daily Yiddish newspaper.

1886      The Jewish Theological Seminary Association is

formed to combat the Reform movement; it begins to operate in 1887.
Yeshivat Etz Chaim is founded as a secondary school for Talmudic study.

1887    Oscar Solomon Straus, lawyer and Jewish communal leader, is appointed by President Grover Cleveland as minister to Turkey.

1888    The Jewish Publication Society of America is founded.
A group of East European congregations in New York City brings Rabbi Jacob Joseph from Vilna to serve as chief rabbi of New York.

1889    Isaac Mayer Wise founds the Central Conference of American Rabbis and becomes its first president.

1891    The Baron de Hirsch Fund is created to help absorb East European Jewish immigrants in America.

1892    The American Jewish Historical Society is founded.

1893    The Educational Alliance is established on New York City's Lower East Side.

1894    The Union Prayer Book is published by the Central Conference of American Rabbis.
The Immigration Restriction League is founded.

1896    Theodor Herzl publishes *Der Judenstaat* ("The Jewish State").

1897    The First Zionist Congress meets in Basel.
The Jewish Labor Bund is founded in Vilna.

The *Jewish Daily Forward*, a Yiddish Socialist daily, begins publishing in New York City.

The Rabbi Isaac Elchanon Theological Seminary (RIETS), the first Orthodox institution for advanced Talmud study, is established in New York City.

1898 The Union of Orthodox Jewish Congregations is founded.

The Federation of American Zionists is organized.

1900 Isaac Mayer Wise dies.

The International Ladies Garment Workers Union is formed by the amalgamation of seven locals.

The Workmen's Circle (*Arbeter Ring*) is founded.

1902 The Jewish Theological Seminary of America is reorganized and begins functioning under the presidency of Dr. Solomon Schechter.

Abraham Cahan becomes editor in chief of the *Jewish Daily Forward*, a post that he holds until his death in 1951.

1903 In April a two-day pogrom in Kishenev, Bessarabia, then in Russia, leaves forty-seven Jews murdered, thousands wounded, plundered, and homeless.

1904 The Russo-Japanese war breaks out.

1905 The *Jewish Encyclopedia* is published in New York City, the first major work of Jewish scholarship produced by American Jews.

The repression after the unsuccessful revolution in Russia leads to a new wave of pogroms under the instigation of the anti-Semitic Black Hundreds.

On December 4 over one hundred thousand New Yorkers parade to demonstrate their sorrow and outrage over the Russian pogroms.

*1906*  Jewish students form the Harvard Menorah Society, the first Jewish collegiate association.
On November 11 the American Jewish Committee is founded.

*1909*  The New York Kehillah is organized, with Rabbi Judah L. Magnes at its head.
The shirtwaist makers, mostly Jewish girls and women, go on strike in what is called "The Uprising of the Twenty Thousand."
The Hebrew Sheltering and Immigrant Aid Society (HIAS) is formed by a merger of two organizations aiding Jewish immigrants.

*1910*  The first secular Yiddish schools are established by the Labor Zionist movement.
In July sixty thousand cloakmakers of the ILGWU go out on strike for two months; Jewish communal leaders mediate an end to the strike by concluding a "Protocol of Peace."

*1911*  In March fire breaks out at the Triangle Shirtwaist Factory, a typical sweatshop, taking 146 lives.
The United States abrogates a commercial treaty with Russia because it discriminated against Jews; the three-year campaign against the treaty was led by the American Jewish Committee.

*1912*  The Young Israel is founded on the Lower East Side in New York.
Hadassah, the Women's Zionist Organization of America, is founded by Henrietta Szold.

1913        The Anti-Defamation League is established.
            The Intercollegiate Menorah Association is
            formed.
            The United Synagogue of America, the congrega-
            tional arm of the Conservative movement, is
            founded.

1914        The Great War begins in August.
            Meyer London, a Jewish Socialist, is elected to
            Congress from New York's East Side.
            The American Jewish Joint Distribution Commit-
            tee is organized.
            The Amalgamated Clothing Workers of America is
            formed.

1915        Leo Frank, arrested in Atlanta in 1913 for allegedly
            murdering a girl, is kidnapped from prison
            and lynched.
            The Ku Klux Klan is revived.
            Yeshivat Etz Chaim and RIETS merge formally as
            RIETS.

1916        The Workmen's Circle establishes secular Yiddish
            schools as supplementary afternoon schools to
            public education.
            President Woodrow Wilson appoints Louis Dem-
            bitz Brandeis to the Supreme Court.
            On May 13 Sholom Aleichem, the noted Yiddish
            writer, dies in New York.
            The Jewish Publication Society publishes the Bible
            in what has since become the standard English
            version of the Masoretic text.

1917        In March revolutionary forces in Russia overthrow
            the czarist regime and establish a democratic
            order.
            The National Jewish Welfare Board is organized to

serve the religious needs of American Jews in the armed forces.

The British government issues the Balfour Declaration on November 2.

On November 7 the Bolsheviks seize power in Russia.

1918     The Federation of American Zionists is reorganized as the Zionist Organization of America.

On November 11 an armistice is declared and the war is ended.

On November 18 the American Jewish Congress, an ad hoc body to deal with the problems of Jewish rights in postwar Europe, elects officers to represent Jewish interests at the Paris Peace Conference.

Mordecai M. Kaplan establishes the Jewish Center in New York as a synagogue center.

Maurice Schwartz organizes the Jewish Art Theatre.

1919     The Treaty of Versailles is signed by the Germans in June.

The Covenant of the League of Nations is included in the Treaty of Versailles.

On November 19 the U.S. Senate refuses to ratify the Covenant.

The Rabbinical Assembly of America is formed as the central body of Conservative rabbis.

1920     Henry Ford's *Dearborn Independent* begins publishing anti-Semitic propaganda, including the *Protocols of the Elders of Zion.*

1921     The U.S. Congress enacts restrictive immigration legislation.

Nicola Sacco and Bartolomeo Vanzetti are convicted of murder. (They are electrocuted in 1927.)

1922    The American Jewish Congress is reconstituted as a permanent organization.
        The Jewish Education Association is formed in New York to improve the status of Jewish education.

1923    The first B'nai B'rith Hillel Foundation is established at the University of Illinois at Urbana.

1924    President Calvin Coolidge signs into law the Immigration Act of 1924, with its national-origins clause, thus effectively halting mass immigration into the United States.

1927    Henry Ford ceases publishing anti-Semitic propaganda and publicly expresses his regrets for having done so.

1928    Yeshiva College is established as an outgrowth of RIETS.
        The National Conference of Christians and Jews is formed to eliminate prejudice from American society.

1929    The stock-market crash of October leads to a severe economic depression.

1932    President Herbert Hoover appoints Benjamin Nathan Cardozo to the Supreme Court.

1933    Franklin Delano Roosevelt becomes the thirty-third President of the United States.
        Herbert H. Lehman becomes governor of New York.

Adolf Hitler becomes head of the German government on January 30.

1934     The Jewish Labor Committee is organized.

1937     The Central Conference of American Rabbis, meeting in Columbus, Ohio, adopts a new program, superseding the Pittsburgh Platform, that is more traditional in the observance of Judaism and conciliatory toward Zionism.

1938     In July an international conference meets at Evian, initiated by President Roosevelt to help the resettlement of persecuted Jews and political refugees, but it accomplishes little.

1939     President Roosevelt appoints Felix Frankfurter to the Supreme Court.
The United Jewish Appeal is founded as a permanent organization.
In May the British government issues its restrictive White Paper on Palestine.
On August 24 Nazi Germany and the Soviet Union sign a nonaggression pact.
On September 1 Germany invades Poland and the Second World War begins. On September 3, England and France declare war on Germany. On September 17 the Soviet Union invades Poland and by the end of the year the partition of Poland is completed.

1940     The YIVO Institute for Jewish Research (formerly Yiddish Scientific Institute—YIVO) moves its headquarters from Vilna, Poland, to New York City.

1941     On June 22 Germany invades its former ally, the Soviet Union.

On December 7 the Japanese bomb Pearl Harbor, and the next day Congress declares war on Japan. On December 11 Germany and Italy declare war on the United States.

1942     American Zionists adopt the Biltmore Program, calling for the establishment of a Jewish state in Palestine.

In June reports of the mass murder of the European Jews reach London.

In July thousands of Jews in New York and in other cities in the United States hold demonstrations and commemorations about the fate of the European Jews.

In November the State Department releases long-held information on the murder of the European Jews. Meetings are convened throughout the United States. On December 8 a Jewish delegation calls upon President Roosevelt.

On December 17 the Allied nations issue a declaration on the German policy of murdering the Jews.

1943     In March New York Jews organize a demonstration in Madison Square Garden.

On April 19 the Jews in the Warsaw Ghetto begin their doomed uprising against the Germans. On the same day delegates of the British and American governments open a conference in Bermuda to consider ways of rescuing European Jews, but nothing is accomplished.

On August 29 the American Jewish Conference is convened, adopting a rescue program that concentrates on Palestine.

1944     President Roosevelt establishes the War Refugee Board.

Torah Umesorah (National Society for Hebrew Day Schools) is organized.

1945    President Roosevelt dies on April 12; Harry S. Truman becomes President.

The United Nations Conference on International Organization meets in San Francisco April 25 to draft the charter of the United Nations Organization.

Adolf Hitler commits suicide on April 30.

The war in Europe ends on May 8 (V-E Day) and in the Pacific on August 15 (V-J Day).

The trial of the major German war criminals opens in Nuremberg on November 20; it is concluded October 1, 1946.

President Truman issues a directive to facilitate the admission to the United States of displaced persons.

1947    On November 29 the UN General Assembly votes in favor of a plan to partition Palestine into independent Jewish and Arab states.

1948    On May 14 Israel declares itself an independent state and is recognized by the United States and the Soviet Union.

On May 15 the British withdraw from Palestine and the Arab armies invade Israel.

The Displaced Persons Act authorizes the admission of over two hundred thousand European refugees to the United States.

1949    Armistices are arranged between Israel and each of the five belligerent Arab states.

Brandeis University is established at Waltham, Massachusetts, as the first secular and nonsectarian university in the United States under Jewish auspices.

| 1952 | The Federal Republic of Germany signs an agreement to pay Israel and Jewish institutions outside Israel $822 million as their "obligation to make moral and material amends" for the murder of the European Jews. |
|------|---|
| 1953 | On March 7 Joseph Stalin dies; his death brings a halt to the major anti-Semitic campaign he had launched. |
| 1954 | American Jews mark the tercentenary of Jewish settlement in the United States with a yearlong program of activities with cultural and educational emphases. |
| 1956 | Nikita Khrushchev denounces Stalin and his policies in a "secret" report delivered at the Twentieth Congress of the Soviet Union's Communist party in February.<br>An uprising in Hungary is suppressed by Soviet troops.<br>Israel, provoked by Arab threats, invades Egyptian territory and is joined by England and France, but all withdraw their forces under U.S. and Soviet pressure. |
| 1960 | Adolf Eichmann is captured in Argentina by Israeli agents and brought to Israel.<br>John F. Kennedy is elected President of the United States, the first Catholic ever to win the presidency. |
| 1961 | Adolf Eichmann's trial opens in Jerusalem on April 11 and concludes on December 15. |
| 1963 | Americans of all races and religions join in the March on Washington for Jobs and Freedom.<br>President Kennedy is assassinated on November |

22; Lyndon B. Johnson assumes the presidency.

1965    A new Immigration Act is passed by Congress, abolishing the quota system based on national origins.
Vatican Council II adopts a declaration on the Catholic Church's relations to the Jews.

1967    During the summer, blacks riot in dozens of large cities in the United States.
Israel wins the Six-Day War against its Arab enemies.

1968    The New York City teachers' strike exacerbates tensions between Jews and blacks.

1973    The Yom Kippur War begins when Egypt and Syria attack Israel. The UN arranges a cease-fire on October 22, after Israeli forces have surrounded the Egyptians; prisoners are exchanged in November.

1975    On November 10 the UN General Assembly adopts a resolution declaring that "zionism" is "a form of racism and racial discrimination."

1976    Saul Bellow wins the Nobel prize for literature.
Jimmy Carter is elected President of the United States.

1978    Isaac Bashevis Singer wins the Nobel prize for literature.
Anwar Sadat writes an "Open Letter to American Jews," asking them to assume "a historic responsibility" in creating peace between Israel and Egypt.
On September 5, Sadat, Menahem Begin, and

Jimmy Carter start a summit conference at the American presidential retreat at Camp David.

*1979*   On March 26 Carter, Sadat, and Begin sign the peace treaty between Egypt and Israel and the United States–Israel memorandum of agreement.

After Andrew Young's resignation from the State Department because of an unauthorized meeting with the PLO, black leaders issue an angry statement expressing their hostility against American Jews.

# SUGGESTIONS
# FOR FURTHER READING

THE LIST OF BOOKS that follows is a small selection from the rich literature about the Jews of America. Each reader can pursue his own interests in the wide range of memoirs and biography of famous and not-so-famous American Jews; in the many community histories of large and small American cities where Jews live; in the numerous congregational histories that chart the course of their institutions; and in the novels, short stories, and poetry about the Jewish experience in America. This list is just a beginning.

Adler, Selig. *The Isolationist Impulse: Its Twentieth-Century Reaction* (New York, 1966).

Antonovsky, Aaron, ed. *The Early Jewish Labor Movement in the United States* (New York, 1961).

Baron, Salo W. *Steeled by Adversity: Essays and Addresses on American Jewish Life* (Philadelphia, 1971).

Belth, Nathan C. *A Promise to Keep: A Narrative of the American Encounter with Anti-Semitism* (New York, 1979).

Cahan, Abraham. *The Education of Abraham Cahan* (New York, 1969).

———. *The Rise of David Levinsky* (New York, 1912).

Cohen, Naomi W. *A Dual Heritage* (Philadelphia, 1969).

———. *American Jews and the Zionist Idea* (New York, 1975).

———. *Not Free to Desist* (Philadelphia, 1972).

Davis, Moshe. *The Emergence of Conservative Judaism: The Historical School in 19th Century America* (Philadelphia, 1963).

Dinnerstein, Leonard. *Antisemitism in the United States* (New York, 1971).

———. *The Leo Frank Case* (New York, 1968).

Feingold, Henry. *The Politics of Rescue: The Roosevelt Administration and the Holocaust, 1938–1945* (New Brunswick, N.J., 1970).

———. *Zion in America: The Jewish Experience from Colonial Times to the Present* (New York, 1974).

Gartner, Lloyd P., ed. *Jewish Education in the United States: A Documentary History* (New York, 1969).

Glazer, Nathan. *American Judaism,* 2nd ed. (Chicago, 1972).

Gold, Michael. *Jews without Money* (New York, 1965).

Gordon, A. I. *Jews in Suburbia* (Boston, 1959).

Goren, Arthur A. *New York Jews and the Quest for Community: The Kehilla Experiment, 1908–1922* (New York, 1970).

Halpern, Ben. *The American Jew: A Zionist Analysis* (New York, 1956).

Higham, John. *Send These to Me: Jews and Other Immigrants in Urban America* (New York, 1975).

———. *Strangers in the Land: Patterns of American Nativism, 1860–1925* (New Brunswick, N.J., 1955).

Howe, Irving. *World of Our Fathers* (New York, 1976).

Janowsky, Oscar I., ed. *The American Jew: A Reappraisal* (Philadelphia, 1964).

Klaperman, Gilbert. *The Story of Yeshiva University: The First Jewish University in America* (New York, 1969).

Lurie, H. L. *A Heritage Affirmed: The Jewish Federation Movement in America* (Philadelphia, 1961).

Mann, Arthur. *The One and the Many: Reflections on the American Identity* (Chicago, 1979).

Reznikoff, Charles, ed. *Louis Marshall: Champion of Liberty: Selected Papers and Addresses* (Philadelphia, 1957).

Ribalow, Harold U., ed. *Autobiographies of American Jews* (Philadelphia, 1973).

Ringer, Benjamin. *The Edge of Friendliness: A Study of Jewish-Gentile Relations* (New York, 1967).

Rischin, Moses. *The Promised City: New York Jews, 1870–1914* (Cambridge, Mass., 1962).

Sanders, Ronald. *The Downtown Jews: Portraits of an Immigrant Generation* (New York, 1969).

Sklare, Marshall. *America's Jews* (New York, 1971).

———. *Conservative Judaism: An American Religious Movement*, new ed. (New York, 1972).

——— and Greenblum, Joseph. *Jewish Identity on the Suburban Frontier* (New York, 1967).

Steinberg, Stephen. *The Academic Melting Pot: Catholics and Jews in American Higher Education* (New York, 1974).

Teller, Judd L. *Strangers and Natives: The Evolution of the American Jews from 1921 to the Present* (New York, 1968).

Urofsky, Melvin I. *American Zionism from Herzl to the Holocaust* (New York, 1975).

———. *We Are One! American Jewry and Israel* (New York, 1978).

# INDEX